Praise for *Tales*

"Dr. Filos paints vivid pictures of pet parents and the many life lessons that they and their 'fur babies' can teach us."

—MELINDA G. McCALL, DVM, author of *Driving Home Naked: And Other Misadventures of a Country Veterinarian*

"Dr. Dawn educates readers on what it means to be a real vet with real stories of pets of all sizes and species. Her entertaining stories will connect with pet lovers and all those who like a good book and a fun read."

—STEVE SILBIGER, author of *The Ten-Day MBA*

"A wonderful read—Dr. Dawn engages the reader with her story-telling prowess. *Tales of a Pet Vet* is a must-read for every person who owns a pet and for every person who wants to work in the animal industry."

—LAURA C. LEFKOWITZ, DVM,
author of *Bite Me: Tell-All Tales of an Emergency Veterinarian*

"Whether she's facing a vicious dog, a recalcitrant cat, or nutty pet parents, Dawn's stories are relatable and entertaining."

—MARY CARLSON, DVM, author of *Drinking from the Trough: A Veterinarian's Memoir*

"A charming and delightful memoir. This book is filled with real-life sweet, humorous, goofy, heartbreaking, and extraordinary stories. Veterinarians, future veterinarians, and animal lovers will all find value in this book."

—DR. EVE HARRISON, VMD, CVA, CVPM, CCFP,
host of *The House Call Vet Café* podcast

TALES OF A PET VET

STORIES FROM THE CLINIC AND HOUSE CALLS

DR. DAWN FILOS

SHE WRITES PRESS

Published 2024
Printed in the United States of America

Print ISBN: 978-1-64742-758-0
E-ISBN: 978-1-64742-759-7
Library of Congress Control Number: 2024909914

For information, address:
She Writes Press
1569 Solano Ave #546
Berkeley, CA 94707

Interior design and typeset by Katherine Lloyd, The DESK

She Writes Press is a division of SparkPoint Studio, LLC.

The names of pets, clients, and other persons, with the exception of family, have been changed to protect their identity and privacy. All those disguised or otherwise have provided permission for their mention in this book.

This book is dedicated to my family,
who patiently listened to these stories for decades.

And of course, to my beloved patients,
who touched my heart.

CONTENTS

INTRODUCTION

One morning last spring I started my day as usual, reviewing the list of house calls on the schedule. As a mobile veterinarian, my day was full of visits, including a stop at a breeder's farm to examine fifteen Cavalier King Charles spaniel puppies. Puppies always brought a lot of fun, but that morning's schedule and accompanying notes told me that the pups' wellness visit was going to have to wait until the end of the day.

The rest of my stops read like a script from an episode of a pet ER show on Animal Planet. The first appointment was urgent. Mabel, a Labradoodle, had gotten her paw caught between the iron scrolls of a barstool. Her owner, Mrs. Lerner, had frantically described a bloody, chaotic scene. Poor Mabel was howling and gnawing at the paw, trying to escape. My answering service had written in all capital letters, *PLEASE SEE FIRST*, in case I hadn't already discerned that Mabel was the patient most in need of my help. Before I continued reading the list, I called out to my assistant to contact the local police about borrowing their Jaws of Life tool—*again*.

My second stop also involved a limb injury, but this one was much more mysterious. Gidget, a healthy Jack Russell terrier, had been left home alone the day before while her owner worked a double shift. Gidget was able to use the dog door to go outside and relieve herself. When her owner returned at the end of the day, Gidget was missing a leg. The intake notes indicated that the owner could not locate the limb out in the yard, but there was a small area of blood near the fence. Other than the missing limb, Gidget did not seem to be in any distress.

Appointment number three was with a fifty-pound American pit bull terrier named Gandhi. He had eaten $500 worth of marijuana. As I gathered my supplies and headed out to the car to start my rounds, I wondered if the marijuana had been baked into brownies. I was worried about chocolate toxicity as much as the effects of the weed itself.

My last stop before I checked on those Cavalier pups was at a household that owned seven cats. Their owner had discovered vomit with fur and blood in it, and the pet hamster, Beluga, was missing from the Habitrail. The owner wasn't sure which feline had done away with the hamster and wanted them all checked. While I was there, she was also requesting a hoof trim on her two pigs.

So there you have it! A "typical" day in the life of a vet who makes house calls.

BECOMING A HOUSE-CALL VET

I've been a vet for over thirty years, working mainly with companion animals such as dogs and cats. A small percentage of my patients have been more exotic species, including rabbits, guinea pigs, lizards, snakes, and birds.

I began my house-call practice nine years ago. Working in pets' home environments has given me diagnostic advantages over my colleagues who see patients in veterinary clinics. Every pet is more relaxed on its home turf than in an unfamiliar, multi-scented, overstimulating veterinary hospital. Pet owners are also more at ease and forthright at home. And I get to see firsthand how the pets' surroundings contribute to their symptoms and imagine how they could be adjusted to accommodate the pet's needs. On a house call, I can glean in seconds what's needed, be it additional litter boxes, orthopedic beds, gated stairways, or smaller cups to measure dinner. The client and I save the time and effort we would otherwise spend attempting to conjure up this mental picture in the office.

This book traces my path from starting out as a young animal lover through three decades of studying and practicing veterinary medicine: I began working in clinics and hospitals, then later moved on to my house-call practice, and now I'm back in clinics again as a relief vet. These pages include many stories of the colorful patients and pet owners I have met along the way. Not a single day in the last thirty years was boring.

In *Tales of a Pet Vet: Stories from the Clinic and House Calls*, you will read about my successes and harder times. You'll meet my eccentric family of animal lovers and hear some wacky anecdotes of clients who went to extremes out of love and devotion to their pets. Anyone who has ever lived with or loved an animal will relate to these stories, which provide a backstage pass to the trials, emotions, and reality of life as a veterinarian. There are a lot of us animal lovers. The American Veterinary Medical Association's (AVMA) most recently published study found 65.1 percent of US households have dogs and 46.5 percent have cats. The estimated dog population is 89.7 million, and cats come in at 58.3 million (AVMA 2022).

My clients take their pet ownership responsibilities seriously. Pets sometimes function as substitutes for family or children, and are referred to by nicknames such as "fur babies," or "four-legged soulmates." The societal shift from pet ownership to "pet parenting" is reflected in the myriad ways we now pamper, spoil, and entertain our adored companions. We strive to provide them with top-notch veterinary care, diets, and forms of stimulation such as play groups and deluxe boarding facilities, most of which were nonexistent three decades ago.

In 2022, the United States spent an estimated $136.8 billion on pets, depending on the surveys cited (American Veterinary Medical Association 2022; Megna 2022; Forbes 2023; American Pet Products Association 2023). The American Pet Products Association (APPA) estimated US spending on pets at $123.6 billion in 2021 (Megna 2023).

Households spent a mean of $354 on veterinary care in 2020. Pet pamperers (who consider pets their world and money no object) spent the most at the vet—$490—compared to casual caretakers (people with several pets who need valuable services at the right price), who spent $138 (Burns 2022).

In the house-call setting, I experience plenty of drama, and I always expect the unexpected. I have been urinated, defecated, and vomited upon; I've been bitten, scratched, and humped. I've chased after and been chased by my patients. I have treated pets in powder rooms, in and under beds, atop washing machines, and in garages, carports, and minivans.

While I explore some serious topics and tell some poignant tales here, the book is also filled with humor. People and animals can be funny, and I often poke fun at myself as a pet parent, sharing the antics of my own pets as well as my clients. I have devoted more hours than I want to admit to searching through vomit and bowel movements for valuables clients wanted me to retrieve. And only in a home setting would I be interrupted during an exam by Amazon's Alexa asking if she should continue listing the most popular sex toys on the market.

It may not have been a glamorous life, but it has been full of extraordinary events. *Tales of a Pet Vet* is my attempt to put into words the wonder of our deep bonds with pets and the joy and delight every day with them brings. I hope you enjoy reading about my escapades as much as I've enjoyed living them.

Dawn Filos
February 2, 2023

CHAPTER I

THE MAKING OF AN ANIMAL LOVER

I trace my decision to become a veterinarian to when my dog Jeepers, a miniature poodle, broke his hip and hind leg. I recall the day distinctly. It was a rainy morning, and for me, the first day of first grade. Clad in my Catholic school uniform, which was new enough to feel scratchy and unfamiliar, I was nervous about the upcoming school year. I looked out the kitchen window and watched Jeepers loping up the street, returning from his morning walk. Just before he reached the front yard, I heard the screech of tires. As I looked on in horror, Jeepers was struck and thrown several feet.

The distraught driver came out to check on him and wailed loudly, thinking Jeepers was dead.

My mother and I raced out to our beloved pet. Mom swaddled Jeepers in a blanket and sped off to our veterinarian while a friend's mother drove me to school.

Jeepers' injuries were extensive. He was treated by a surgical specialist at the famous Animal Medical Center in nearby New York City.

The recuperation process cemented my interest in the veterinary field. I still recall specific details from fifty years ago, such as the blue-and-pink pattern on the baby playpen where Jeepers rested in our driveway, yard, and kitchen as he healed. I was present for all the follow-up trips to the vet center, where I met doctors and nurses who, like us, didn't give a second thought to investing such effort and cost into healing a four-legged family member.

I now appreciate just how unusual my wonderful family was, and the extraordinary level of devotion we showed to our pets. I am who I am as a veterinarian because of the animal lovers in my extended family and am forever grateful for their example.

My family could be described as blended. Usually this implies stepparents, stepbrothers, and stepsisters. For me, it meant a mix of my mother, an animal lover, and my father, a Greek immigrant who wasn't raised with indoor animals.

For many of my formative years, my maternal grandparents lived next door with Sheba, a German shepherd. I often referred to my grandmother as a German shepherd breeder. But Sheba was not well-bred. Nor were her offspring. Some of Sheba's puppies bore a strong resemblance to a neighbor's intact male Rottweiler—they were mostly black and short-haired, with blocky heads—making their shepherd lineage highly suspect.

Sheba gave birth to several dozen lovely pups. My siblings, cousins, and I took turns at swinging them around in large circles to "clear their lungs" just after they were born. Not until decades later did I realize this home obstetrics practice had fallen out of favor, at least in the opinion of my veterinary professors. It's likely few would recommend warming the newborns in the oven either, but that's what we learned to do as we whelped them in preparation to send them off to their forever homes.

A short list of kittens came to our house and then went to my aunt's home, as my mother proved allergic to cats. Mom repeatedly refused to believe a cat lover such as herself could be allergic to the objects of her affection. Nonetheless, with time, several doses of Claritin, and the advice of an immunologist, she gave up her dream of being a cat mom.

My mother converted my father into a dog lover with a constant stream of large dogs—Irish setters, a Rottweiler who saved my brother's life in NYC during an attempted robbery, and a German shepherd, also named Sheba. Jeepers, and Sugar, a Maltese, marked a preference shift to small white breeds.

We also had a myna bird named Pepper, who had a huge vocabulary. Later, my brother had an African grey parrot who used profanity extensively. My sister is a bird aficionado, and one of her birds screams obscenities at me whenever we try to talk on the phone.

With time, our family became well-known animal lovers, at least locally. My mother hosted an infamous dog birthday/Halloween party for our Irish setter, Sampson. Mom required all four-legged guests to arrive in costume. The event was well attended, and we made the front page of the *Jersey Journal* newspaper. It was sometime in the midseventies, should you want to look it up. If you find it, please forward a copy to me.

Unfortunately, a basset hound, promiscuously dressed in a miniskirt and evidently in heat, got a little extra attention. Sixty-three days later, she and her family welcomed a litter of puppies.

When I was twelve, we adopted Willie, a woolly monkey. My mother found him in a sketchy pet store in Miami. I suspect he was illegally smuggled into the country. He weighed about twelve pounds and wore cute, colorful baby diapers with a hole cut out for his tail.

I have a vivid memory of our exciting return trip home and landing at Newark airport with Willie. At baggage claim, it was announced that everyone should pay close attention to the arrival of a very special guest on our luggage carousel. Willie wore a teal turtleneck sweater that had somehow gotten pulled up and covered his head. Hundreds of people looked askance as he emerged screaming—a headless, arm-flailing, ET-like creature riding the luggage carousel.

Willie bonded with my father. He loved to nap on Dad's chest on our plastic slipcovered couches. He adored ice cream, and fought with my younger sister, Faith, as if they were siblings.

Our family achieved legendary status as crazy pet lovers when I took Willie to school to fulfill an assignment to share something interesting about myself in class. Willie was certainly interesting. St. Mary's Catholic School didn't know what to do when I showed up with him. My mother convinced them to allow not just my fifth-grade class to meet him, but the entire school.

Sadly, later that year, I returned home from school one day and Willie was gone. My mother told me he was not well-suited to life in northern New Jersey and had been sent to live on a farm in Pennsylvania. After I had lived in Pennsylvania for decades without ever seeing a single monkey farm, it finally sank in that Willie had met a much darker fate. My mother confirmed that he had died of pneumonia. A New Jersey basement in the winter was not an ideal environment for a growing monkey.

Today, I can't imagine that a parade of hundreds of children would be allowed to pet a monkey, at least not in the public schools where my three children went. And honestly, as a veterinarian, the thought of stressing out a pet with exposure to hordes of excited, groping children makes me cringe. But at my twenty-fifth school reunion, classmates still recalled the thrill of meeting Willie. None of them were surprised I became a veterinarian.

CATS GONE WILD

My childhood primed me for my career and the colorful, wonderful families I would meet, many of whom reminded me of my own. My favorite story is about another eccentric family, to whom I completely related. They would have fit right in with my relatives.

One busy evening at work, I got a call from several people who were simultaneously yelling into the phone. I could barely make out the words, but "fighting" and "bloodshed" were among them. I instructed them to come in right away.

Shortly after, five people walked in with seven cats among them, all of whom were quietly napping in their respective carriers. I was confused. Were these the same people I'd spoken with just thirty minutes ago?

In the treatment area, I assessed the cats' heart rates and neurological status. Other than being sleepy and unusually calm, they were fine; all of them were hydrated and in no obvious imminent physical distress or danger. Two were my patients, Felix and Oscar. Their pet parents, Shirley and Sherry, had lavished these lucky cats with gifts and the best veterinary care for the many years I knew them.

Oscar wore a bow tie, which intrigued me. I soon learned Shirley and Sherry had hosted a "catsinera" birthday fiesta for fifteen-year-old Oscar that evening. This explained the small sombrero in Felix's carrier.

The "catsinera" guest list included five kitty acquaintances, all of whom enjoyed the elaborate Martha Stewart–themed decor and buffet. While the pet parents sipped "meow-garitas," the cats converged upon the buffet table with its tuna "cat-serole" and "kitty lasagna," both of which were topped with catnip resembling green grated cheese.

The combination of cats and catnip always makes for an unusual day at work. Catnip is a plant in the Lamiaceae family, which includes basil, mint, thyme, lavender, rosemary, and oregano. It's often referred to as "weed for cats," even though cannabis and catnip are unrelated species, perhaps because the feline response to catnip resembles the effect of intoxicants on people. They first become playful, then agitated and excited, and finally they fall asleep.

While cats sometimes ingest catnip, they prefer to roll in it and smell it. It contains nepetalactone, an essential oil that, when sniffed, travels to receptors in the amygdala, also known as the emotional or "happy" center of the brain, and causes euphoria. It also makes connections in the hypothalamus, the area of the brain that, in part, controls the impulses to eat and mate. About half of all cats are unfazed by the plant. But the behavior of those who are affected can be alarming for unaware pet parents.

Evidently, what can only be described as a melee ensued at the lasagna tray. It soon escalated into a "Sharks vs. Jets" version of *West Side Story*, but with claws.

Sherry's comment, "It all happened so fast!" didn't help me determine who was bitten, or where on their bodies they were injured.

Shirley soberly admitted, "After they fought, they all got extremely tired, and we thought they had been drugged. That's when we called you, Dr. Filos. What could have happened?"

Mistake number one: Having a cat party. It's never a good idea. Ever. Not even in your own home with your own cats. And why go a step further and stuff your pet into a carrier and then release them into a strange home?

Mistake number two: Exposing a group of perplexed, stressed cats to a tray of drugs they cannot resist and that will make them do stupid things. It's comparable to hosting a party for a bunch of four-year-olds in your dining room with white decor and encouraging them to go wild with fingerpaint after you've given them sodas.

Mistake number three: Calling attention to Oscar's "cat-sinera" and celebrating his fifteenth birthday. If you converted cat years into people years, that would make him pretty damn old! The golden years are not the time to recreate a scene from a Cheech and Chong movie.

I was able to locate two small bite wounds on two of the cat guests, which I cleaned and treated. All of the patients slept it off and were back to normal by the following morning.

PET PARENTS

Over the last few decades I have watched many clients like Shirley and Sherry morph from pet owners into pet parents. I'm not the only one who has noticed the trend—in response to this shift, the pet food and product industry has exploded with variety. Today's pet parents can choose from a staggering array of services and luxuries now available for these adored members of their families.

Terms like "fur babies" or "fluffy kids" didn't exist twenty years ago. Neither did pet resorts, blueberry dog facials, or dog perfume named Sexy Beast. Now, if money is no object, you can buy a $3,500 cat house, or a $6,000 diamond-studded dog collar. This week, a colleague mentioned clients who purchased their puppy for $40,000. They referred to him as their "pet son." It is difficult to shock me, but this sticker price did.

Now more than ever, we treat our pets as part of the family. There are so many fun ways to pamper them, from diverse experiential activities to a vast variety of diets, toys, and clothing for them.

Among American pet parents:

- Thirty-six percent give their pets a birthday present (me too!).
- Twenty-seven percent have arranged professional pet photography sessions.
- Fifty percent talk to their pets (Burns 2022).

These fun facts hint at several recent trends which demonstrate just how much we love—and some might say obsess about—our pets. I see it every day, which is why I categorized the top seven types of pet parents I see. While intentionally humorous, this list is a fairly accurate summation of how many of us feel about our four-legged "children." You may not refer to yourself as a pet parent or your pet as a "fur baby," but you may still recognize yourself or someone you know in the following depictions.

1. THE DAILY CHRONICLE PET PARENT

Professional pet photography is all the rage. Think of Anne Geddes's beautiful baby photos with infants arranged artfully among flowers, asleep and adorable—but with pets. Newborn dog and cat photo sessions can actually rival Geddes's in quality. I have patients who get yearly "school photos" at their doggie day care, with the same background images and poses my own children bring home from school. I am frequently asked for artist referrals to commission and create pet oil and pastel paintings for families.

Wedding announcements and holiday cards have included pets for years. I've received invitations to pet baby showers, soon after or even before the arrival of the puppy or kitten. Add to this pet birthday parties and weddings, and you have an entire cottage industry that's arisen from our love of pets.

2. THE FASHIONISTA PET PARENT

Pet clothing options are vast and rival the latest issue of *Vogue* in cutting-edge style. Decades ago, I recommended clients shop at Build-A-Bear to find affordable outfits for their small dogs. Now, the sky's the limit: people buy bathing suits, leather bomber jackets, booties, Halloween costumes, and upscale jewelry with price tags higher than the cost of my 1992 wedding.

3. THE FOODIE PET PARENT

Dietary awareness has altered the culinary climate of the planet, and not just for people. We are more aware of the benefits of high-quality ingredients in our diets and are attuned to gluten, grain, or lactose intolerances, to name a few. If you've ever wondered whether your dog eats better than you do, you may be a foodie pet parent. The dog food industry has exploded with options, which can make picking your pet's food an anxiety-riddled experience. Boutique fresh food brands, a new and growing component of the pet food market, have multiplied in number. Their message suggests that feeding pets commercially-made dry kibble is outdated or even bad for their health.

Buyer beware, though. The industry has also taken advantage of our wish to be the best pet parents we can be. Many companies have falsely marketed diets with unsubstantiated claims of health benefits and misrepresentation concealed in clever advertisements intended to mislead well-intentioned consumers. Organic, raw, or kangaroo-meat-based plans are available, for example . . . Ingredient lists should come with a handbook of how to interpret them.

4. THE HELICOPTER PET PARENT

It is now possible to monitor your pets remotely, even while you're at your workplace, with GPS dog-tracking devices. When you hire a dog walker, you may collect data and trace their route to verify that they walked to the dog park and back.

Some of us have left radios on for our pets or said hello to them over an answering machine every now and then. We might play Dog TV or Animal Planet all day for them in our absence. You might even spoil your pets from afar with Petzi, an interactive "treat cam." Microphones on the device allow you to speak to your dogs and even fling treats at them from a dispenser.

5. THE WELL-LIVED/WELL-ROUNDED LIFESTYLE PET PARENT

It's hard to stay abreast of all the new gadgets and experiential enrichments you can offer your pet. It's become like *Keeping Up with the Kardashians*, with luxury pet resorts offering heated beds, personal plasma-screen televisions, in-room doggie massages, and limo-driven excursions to the drive-through at McDonald's. This is the new reality of many fortunate dogs.

You can arrange for in-home veterinary visits, dog sitters, groomers, and even hire someone else to come and clean up after your dog's mess in the yard. Sound and music programs like iCalmPet are specially created and tested for cats and dogs to ease separation anxiety and noise phobias. I have clients who play an eight-hour music video, *Music for Dogs*, on continuous loops to augment their pet's behavioral medications.

The beauty line product selections are dizzying. One high-end boutique sells Dead Sea salts for dog baths and "dog wine" in a corked bottle, while a pianist serenades two- and four-legged shoppers. I once almost bought a product called Aesop Animal Wash Dog Shampoo for forty dollars, available at Bergdorf Goodman, but stopped myself when I realized I wouldn't pay those prices for my own hair products.

Home design firms have developed multipurpose dog rooms and accessories. One of my clients has such a room equipped with a pet shower and a grooming island worthy of a feature spread in *Pet Architectural Digest*, if it existed (perhaps soon enough!).

6. THE SOCIAL MEDIA PET PARENT

I can recall a time when it was unusual for a client to have a Facebook page for their dog or cat. Now it is commonplace for new puppies or kittens to have their own social media accounts. I not only feel compelled to follow the Instagram pages of my patients Maddox and Percy, but I enjoy it. I am amazed at how my friend Laura manages to coax her cooperative, adorable pup Chloe to wear and pose in elaborate outfits.

Personally, I believe dog and cat photos and videos should litter the Internet because I never get enough of them. My own dog is featured prominently on my Dr. Dawn Instagram site. I don't have time to make my dog's images "influencer" quality, but I am impressed by those who do.

7. THE "YES SIR, THAT'S MY FUR BABY" PET PARENT

Long gone are the days when I commented on children who had what I considered "pet names," like Rex and Spike. The situation has reversed, and pet names have become more human. While I think Hazel, Cleo, and Clifford blur the lines and work for both, names like Mary, Kevin, Richard, Heinrich, Dave, Phyllis, Joan, and Leo leave no doubt that these pets are their parents' "children." I miss old names like Sir Barks-A-Lot, Oreo, Cadbury, Jingles, Deeohgee ("dog" spelled out phonetically), and Killer. As a veterinarian, I immediately knew where I stood with Sir Barks-A-Lot and Killer.

I will admit to being a little bit of the daily chronicler (1) and the well-lived/well-rounded lifestyle (5) dog mom, albeit a no-frills version.

ON THE ROAD

Now let's go on a thirty-year (and then some) journey together, beginning with my schooling and continuing throughout my career, as I introduce you to the many patients and pet parents I encountered along the way. These stories run the gamut of scenarios we face with our pets and may stir up emotions and memories you've had with your own pets.

In the next chapter, you'll get a glimpse into the challenges of veterinary school. You'll come with me through some major stumbles, and a few successes, from that time. It was a memorable era, including a madcap mishap when I lost an animal under my care. You won't want to miss reading about that unforgettable, hair-raising day!

CHAPTER 2

BECOMING DR. DAWN

B y the time I went to college, I was set on becoming a veterinarian. As an undergraduate at Rutgers, I majored in biochemistry and plunged into the prerequisites for vet school. In the mid-1980s, there were only twenty-five veterinary schools in the country. None of them were in my home state of New Jersey. Instead, the state had contractual agreements with four other states— Pennsylvania, New York, Ohio, and Alabama— allowing New Jersey residents admittance into veterinary schools and waiving the out-of-state tuition fee. That year, these schools accepted up to twenty-eight students from New Jersey.

I didn't get into veterinary school on my first attempt, so I enrolled in the University of Georgia's master's degree program in physiology. The department was located within the veterinary school, where I studied renal physiology of animals and focused on diseases of the kidneys of dogs and cats, in addition to comparative renal studies of other mammalian species. Then I reapplied to vet school and received one of the fifteen slots allotted to New Jersey residents at the University of Pennsylvania School of Veterinary Medicine.

I loved being on the Philadelphia main campus. I also spent several months in classes and clinics at the large-animal campus, the New Bolton Center, in nearby Kennett Square. There were some memorable moments worth sharing from those four years.

VETERINARY SCHOOL MISHAPS

The first two years of vet school were filled with classwork and labs, such as anatomy and histology. In the third year, we could select elective classes geared to our specific interests, such as small-animal or large-animal medicine, exotics, surgery, etc. Clinical rotations began the summer after the third year and continued through our fourth year.

Over the four years, there were a few times I feared I might not make it to graduation. One weekend in my second year, I had two big finals to prepare for, physiology and pathology. I confused the days and went to campus on Monday prepared for the pathology exam. An hour before the exam, I realized the test that day was in physiology. Panicked, sweaty, and near-hysterical, I sought out Dr. Delluva, the professor who was administering the test.

I opened my mouth to describe what I had done, but my voice would not work. "Doctor Ddddd—" I blurted out. "Doctor Dddd—" I tried again.

Doctor Delluva looked up from the journal she'd been reading and glared at me. "For God's sake, girl, what is it you want to say?"

I gulped and managed to say, "Doctor Delluva, I studied for the wrong exam!" I broke into sobs.

She looked at me, perplexed. "How on earth did you do that?"

"Because I'm a moron!" I wailed. "I confused the pathology and physiology test dates because they both start with *P*." More tears followed.

Dr. Delluva told me to go home, get composed, and return to take the test the following day.

Once I got home, I phoned my fiancé, Dave, and relayed my

woeful tale. He sent me flowers, a very rare extravagance for us, to console me.

Thankfully, I passed both exams and made it to third year.

HOLD ONTO THE REINS

In veterinary school, we spent nearly equal amounts of time focused on large farm animals as on smaller animals like the dogs and cats I primarily wanted to treat. This presented an extra challenge. It required us to learn the differences between, say, a dog's and horse's blood smears. I never intended to work with cows, horses, or especially pigs, but I needed to pass all of my classes and, more importantly, the board exams. I envied Dave, soon to be a medical doctor, who was only required to study one species . . . humans.

The last year of vet school, I rotated through different specialties: emergency medicine, surgery, dermatology, cardiology, neurology, ophthalmology, and internal medicine. I spent most of my time at the small-animal campus and hospital based in Philadelphia.

The large-animal facility was about an hour away, at the New Bolton Center; while we attended classes and worked in the clinics, we stayed in dorms or apartments. I was able to coordinate all three months of large-animal clinic blocks consecutively at New Bolton. I started with medicine, where I was responsible for providing daily treatments and updates to the attending doctor in charge.

There was an unspoken division among my classmates between the small-animal group and the large-animal or "horse people" group. I was firmly in the small-animal group. I tried to keep my lack of horse experience to myself. I had no desire to impress the surgeons or internists with my knowledge or skill. I planned to get through the three months by spending as little time as possible poking around in a cow's rectum with a long glove attempting to locate an ovary. I intended to keep my head low and remain under the radar in clinics. I was there just to obtain enough knowledge to pass the darn boards.

While I had ridden horses for many years as a child, my equine skills were rusty. I rode primarily calm quarter horses accustomed to trotting young girls like me around a dough-nut-shaped area in an enclosed barn. I loved my lessons until the day I chose to ride a spirited horse named Toledo. A loud whinny from the barn caused him to rear up, then manically gallop as I bounced and flailed atop him. I did not have the horsemanship skills necessary to control him. Instead, I latched onto the near-est wooden pole, jumped off Toledo, and twirled down its length with all the grace of the Three Stooges. I pulled splinters from my abraded arms for days.

I never really "got back on the horse" after that incident. It left me with a heavy dose of apprehension and respect for all things equine.

With that past experience, I headed boldly into my large-an-imal clinics. My first assigned case at New Bolton was a Thoroughbred racehorse who suffered from a lung abscess and required many daily treatments. He had been at the medical center a month already and would remain several months after I left. I referred to him as Taz, short for Tasmanian Devil. My initial task was to medicate him. After I ground his pills into a liquid slurry generously flavored with molasses, I squirted the medicine into his mouth. He jerked his stubborn head and neck, leaving me with a patina of sticky back-spit on my head, neck, and clothing.

Next, I was supposed to lead Taz, with a rein, around a small, fenced enclosure adjacent to the barn.

"What a beautiful early September day," I remarked to myself as we walked onto the small pasture. "Hmm . . . this could be fun."

Just then, Taz reared and yanked on the reins and lifted me off the ground. He donkey-kicked and ignored my attempts to calm him. I gasped in horror as he pulled the reins from my hand, jumped the fence, and galloped across the sprawling hundred acres of property around the center.

On my first morning at the center, I had lost a valuable racehorse!

Instantly, wailing sirens blared throughout the facility. People came from all directions, headed directly toward me. Gates were closed at each exit as Taz sped down the hill. Several people ran after him. As I watched the horse escape, I imagined my career also running away from me before it had even gotten started.

In my peripheral vision, I noticed movement to my right. One of the surgeons, atop a horse, galloped past me. When he reached Taz, he straddled his own horse with one leg and Taz with his other, as a rodeo stuntman might, then transferred onto Taz's bare back, collected Taz's reins, and magically took control of him and the situation. It was as if the Lone Ranger had arrived and saved me.

My elation rapidly wore off when a crowd of more than a hundred of my classmates, professors, and surgeons gathered around. Someone asked who was the student designated to be responsible for Taz. I held up my hand, red-faced and mortified.

I was relieved of exercise duty but remained in charge of Taz's medical treatments. Intent on doing a better job treating him, I discovered how to use a twitch—a rope attached to a stick that manipulates a horse's upper lip to distract them. While it may sound cruel, it relaxes a horse by increasing parasympathetic nervous system activity. This enabled me to work with Taz so he understood I was in control. He never fought me again, and I even grew fond of him. I was happy to hear he was discharged a few months later. I never let go of a patient's reins again.

DON'T INTERVIEW WHILE HUNGOVER

In our third year, my classmates and I took time off from clinics to job hunt. Once I spent the weekend with a friend who hosted a party on a Friday night. I had a Saturday morning interview scheduled the next day at a large veterinary hospital in New York.

The pre-interview party proved ill-advised. The combination of too many drinks and staying out much later than I was accustomed to left me bleary-eyed, sleep-deprived, and queasy. Several cups of coffee helped bring me around to alertness as I drove to the interview.

Midway through the interview, the veterinary hospital owner invited me to lunch. We got into his Corvette. En route to the restaurant, he swerved and sped like we were in a NASCAR race. I fought a strong urge to vomit. I no longer cared if I got the job. I rolled down the window and stuck my head out to get some fresh air. My hair blew wildly, and I'm sure I looked ridiculous.

At the restaurant, I picked at my lunch and excused myself to go to the restroom. I grabbed our waitress in a corridor and begged her to remove the rest of my lunch. But it was still there when I returned to the table. I badly wanted to go home and take a nap but realized that the owner was using lunch to conduct the question-and-answer portion of the interview.

I felt so woozy that I slumped in my chair and rested my head on my folded arms on the table. I looked up at the owner and answered his questions. He continued, surely nonplussed by my bizarre behavior.

He described a situation in the hospital when a cat patient needed a blood transfusion. When blood was collected from a different cat with the same blood type, the donor cat collapsed. The practice owner asked me what I would do next.

I mumbled, "Where was the blood?"

He responded in a high-pitched, loud voice, a gleam in his eye, "Why? What do you mean?"

"Did you give the patient the blood yet, or was it still hanging in the bag, ready to be transfused? If not, why not just give it back to the original cat?"

He slammed his hand on the table, making my headache worse. "Exactly! Common sense. That's what a veterinarian needs." He laughed. "Do you know, I've asked this same question for twenty years, and you're the first person to ever answer it correctly?"

I thought, *Great. Are we done? Can we leave now?*

I didn't get the job, no doubt because the owner had time to reflect on my odd behavior. I don't blame him. He said he quite enjoyed our chat but decided to go with someone who had a little more experience under their belt. That was the first and last time I interviewed hungover.

During my senior year, while I was busy in clinics, I also went on more (sober) job interviews and planned my wedding. Before I knew it, I was a vet school graduate, and three weeks later, a wife. My husband, Dave, was just about to enter medical school, so I instantly became the family breadwinner as well.

Veterinarians are not required to do internships or residencies before going into private practice. Most, like me, practiced while we worked at our first jobs. I needed to convince clients I knew what I was doing without any previous training beyond vet school. Confidence comes with experience, and I had neither. It would take years and many opportunities to gain that confidence and become the doctor I am today.

One good decision I made early on didn't seem so at the time. Dave and I had our first argument as a married couple on our wedding night, over which last name I would use professionally. In the end, I chose to keep my married identity separate from my work. I've been happy, in certain situations, to not reveal my profession. Eventually, I settled on simply being called Dr. Dawn. In June 1992, I began my career as such.

Those first few years played out much differently than I'd expected. Many days it felt as if I'd been thrown into the ocean without a life preserver during a terrible storm and I couldn't swim. Am I being too dramatic? You decide as you read Chapter 3.

CHAPTER 3

THE EARLY YEARS

I was not one of those lucky vets with a first boss who mentored me. I didn't hit the jackpot with my second or third bosses, either, so I learned on my feet, independently. My on-the-job training prepared me for a decade of work as a relief vet. A relief veterinarian is similar to a temporary physician, hired to fill in at various hospitals as needed. It meant I was typically the only doctor working a shift while the regular staff was unavailable. Sometimes I was fortunate to have another veterinarian present and I could consult them on cases, but the majority of the time I worked solo. Eventually, this helped me feel brave enough to start and run my own house-call practice.

That confidence took years to arrive, however. I began my training and career much like a newborn foal—on shaky legs. As a recent graduate, I ruminated over every single dose of medication, treatment plan, and interpretation of an X-ray. If I made a mistake, I tended to obsess, full of self-doubt and recrimination. With time I learned from my mistakes and hoped to never repeat them. My confidence was hard-earned.

Veterinarians often beat themselves up if a case doesn't go well. Instead of focusing on the many patients we have healed or treated successfully, we ruminate on the what-ifs. It's human nature to let a rare bad review cause angst despite the positive and kind comments made by the majority of clients. At my worst, insecurities resurface. At my best, I can move past criticism and remind myself it is impossible to please every pet parent. To this day, the animal who suffers an unusual adverse reaction to a medication or experiences a poor outcome still keeps me up at night with worry.

FIRST DAYS AND FAINTING

During my first two jobs, I inadvertently made people faint. I wondered what I was doing to cause this. I guessed that it was due to a combination of my delivery of bad news and the clients being ill, fragile, pregnant, underfed, or queasy at the sight of blood, all of which could and did precipitate lightheadedness. One woman even pinned me between her and the exam table where she stood alongside her pet. She slid down the wall after I broke her fall.

Within the first two months after I graduated, a client passed out during an exam once a week on average. As a joke, the nurses started placing a tray of orange or apple juice, fresh fruit, and smelling salts in the two exam rooms "just in case."

While the staff thought it humorous, I saw it as a visual reminder that I was awful at my job. The police and paramedics were beginning to wonder what was going on at our clinic. In addition to worrying about making correct diagnoses within the allotted fifteen-minute visit (often an impossibility), I was equally focused on assuring proper airflow in the exam rooms. I added fans and made sure there were enough chairs available for each client in the room in the event that someone went down.

The fainting curse followed me to my second job. Once, while I treated a hemorrhaging wound on a dog's leg, his owner passed out and landed headfirst on a metal desk. He left a dent in the desk. I located catheters, a fluid line, and emergency medication needed to treat the dog while the receptionist called the police. I had already learned at my last job that the authorities needed to be notified when someone collapsed.

WHAT YOU SEE IS WHAT YOU GET

Some days I did a better job at impersonating a seasoned, trustworthy veterinarian than others, and some clients were better at hiding their disappointment at meeting me than others. Early on, several clients asked if I was old enough to be a vet. Others felt more comfortable with my boss, a male vet. Nothing boosted my confidence faster than being asked to run my diagnosis by an associate, "just to be sure."

I quickly improved my delivery, however, by using direct eye contact, speaking in succinct sentences, and eliminating any words that could suggest indecision or waffling, such as "I think," "I am pretty sure," and "It seems," etc.

Still, there were those special few who were downright adamant about not seeing me, and insisted on working with their favorite, longtime vet. Their feelings were completely valid, and I often felt relief at having the schedule free up a bit when they rescheduled. More often, though, they were there for an illness check and had no choice but to stick with me. Eventually, I'd win them over by successfully treating their pets.

Or, very occasionally, I would not. One pet owner was so impolite that I put aside my own manners and let him have it. I grew up with eight male cousins who'd prepared me to hold my own with men and bullies. This client was just that.

The day was hectic. I was overbooked with a full schedule and two emergency walk-in appointments. The office was short-staffed, with one nurse assistant out sick. I walked in and greeted the client (let's call him Mr. Rude), and his Rottweiler, Butch, who had ingested rat poisoning an hour earlier. I told him

I needed to induce Butch to vomit and was ready to get down to business.

Cutting me off, Mr. Rude bellowed, "Where is Dr. March? I always see Dr. March. I'm not letting you touch my dog. You're too young and wouldn't know how to handle him. Women can't handle big dogs like him, and you look like you just graduated middle school, for God's sake."

"Absolutely, Mr. Rude," I said as evenly as possible. "I'll be back with Dr. March in a jiffy."

I headed to the treatment room in the back of the hospital and prepared the supplies and medication to induce Butch to vomit up the rat poisoning as soon as possible. Part of me wanted to leave Mr. Rude in the room for an hour to fester in his angry misogyny. But I was a professional and took the high road . . . with a twist. I knocked on the door, entered, and introduced myself again as if I hadn't been in just a few minutes earlier. "Hello, I'm Dr. Filos. I'm here to help Butch."

Mr. Rude's eyes bugged as he gaped at me. "Is this some kind of joke? Where's Dr. March? I specifically told you I wanted to see Dr. March, or someone with more experience."

I nodded. "You did. Dr. March isn't here today. The doctors on staff today are me, myself, and I. I'm all set up to take care of Butch. You have two choices: let me do my job and get the poison out of his system, or leave and find another practice with an older, male doctor. But that will waste valuable time that you don't have. So how about you let me and my two X chromosomes do our job, and you can see Dr. March for follow-up if you wish." I shot him a wide grin and held his gaze.

Mr. Rude was annoyed, but he acquiesced with an expression of begrudging admiration that signaled, *I'll be damned. The girl's got some moxie.*

With a flourish, I collected Butch, who sweetly followed me, cooperated for his medication, and promptly spewed vomitus all over my work clogs. I sent the dog and Mr. Rude on their way, changed into the backup pair of shoes every veterinarian must have on hand, and dealt with the rest of my day.

DID YOU FORGET SOMETHING?

Another equally memorable client comes to mind for very different reasons. A few years after graduating, I worked in a busy practice in Philadelphia. One day, while I was eight months pregnant with my first child, I entered an exam room with a sweet, extremely itchy, and flea-infested pit bull named Millie. Millie was accompanied by her owner, a boy in his early twenties, and three of his male friends. They reeked of marijuana, to the extent that it made me wonder if it was unhealthy for my unborn child and me to be in the same room with them.

I tried to expedite the visit, quickly pointing out the fleas and describing steps for treatment. I became frustrated; they were so stoned they couldn't focus and follow my instructions.

Stoner #1 asked several times, "Doc, why is she itching so much?"

"Well, as I said, there are fleas . . . See them here?" I tried to hide my impatience as I repeated myself for the fourth time. "Millie is allergic to them. That's why she's itching."

Stoner #2 jumped in. "Yeah, but how did she scratch herself like that? And why?"

I bit back a sharp retort. "Well, *again*, fleas made her itchy and she scratched herself raw as a result." I pointed to a small red wound on the pit's back. "This is a hot spot. We need to treat it."

Stoner #1 and 3 said together, "Wow. That sucks. But why? How do we make her stop scratching?"

Before I could answer, Stoner #4 felt the need to join the conversation. "Yeah. Poor Millie. What's wrong with her? She keeps scratching."

Oh, dear God. I had to get them out of there. I was getting behind in appointments and really needed the cast of *Dazed and Confused* to leave pronto. "How about I just start treatment and write down everything you need to do next?" I said.

I gave Millie an anti-itch injection and handed the boys a bag of medication and flea treatments to administer at home. They attempted to leave without paying. More accurately, they ran toward the front door, en masse and in slow motion, stopping at intervals to giggle.

I yelled to Mike, the hospital manager, "Help! They're trying to stiff us. Hurry!"

I shuffled over to them as quickly as my ungainly body allowed. Mike and I easily apprehended them in the parking lot, where they stood arguing outside their car.

"Dude, I thought you had the keys," one of them said to Millie's owner.

He shook his head. "No, *you* had the keys."

"Forget anything?" I piped up. I dangled the car keys they had left in the exam room out in front of me. My other hand held Millie's leash. The dog stood alongside me. The boys doubled over in another fit of laughter as if this was hilarious. I admit to being mildly amused too.

We collected payment and did not press charges. All in all, the incident ended on a "high" note.

BITES

Small-animal veterinarians place themselves daily in situations that put them at risk of bite wounds. Many animals scratch and bite out of fear, pain, and stress. It can be difficult to take control of a situation before you get bitten. I've lost sensation in three fingers due to permanent nerve injuries from cat bites.

And I've gotten off easy. I know several veterinarians and veterinary nurses who had career-ending cat bite wounds with more extensive, permanent nerve damage. I also know some who have suffered disfiguring dog bites to their faces and limbs.

Why don't we muzzle every patient? First, muzzling requires getting close to a patient, which puts the veterinarian at risk. Second, imagine how you would feel if a veterinarian muzzled your adorable kitten or puppy on the first or second visit. Besides, some patients do better without muzzles, which don't prevent all bites or scratches anyway. I prefer to use blankets and towels to gently restrain cats, which is a more effective way to protect myself, and it's less stressful to the patients.

Gaining this knowledge took time and experience that I didn't yet have in the first few years of practice. While I still cannot avoid scratches and bites completely, they occurred more frequently in the early days. At my first position, I was bitten on my hand by a twenty-pound cat who escaped from my grip as I returned her to the kennel. (My right middle finger is permanently numb.)

Two days before my wedding, I had finished my exam on a dog who turned as she was led out of the room and bit me on the arm. I needed antibiotics and found Band-Aids to match my off-white bridal gown.

An even scarier incident at that same practice occurred one Sunday evening when I was caring for a Great Dane in a large, gated kennel in the veterinary hospital basement. He had been well-behaved prior. I stooped to collect his food and water bowl. When I stood back up, he got up on his hind limbs behind me and placed both front paws on my shoulders, pinning me to the now-closed kennel gate. I felt his breath hot and heavy as he snarled at my neck. I fought back panic as I tried to distract him with food. Had it ended another way, I might have been there for hours and could have bled to death before someone found me. I no longer go into kennels with dogs alone in the hospital at night.

Even animals who have never reacted aggressively may do so at some point. I once bent over a well-behaved German short-haired pointer to listen to his heart and inadvertently threatened him with a dominant posture. Without a growl or any other sign of warning, he bit me near my left eyebrow, dangerously close to my eye. It happened so fast I jumped all the way to the opposite side of the room from the shock and adrenaline rush.

I had not yet registered pain, and I asked my assistant, who was staring at me in horror, "Did I just get bit? Am I bleeding?"

She fainted.

I took that as a yes, and we both went to the emergency room. Luckily, I didn't have a fracture of the orbit, the thin bone surrounding the eye socket. But I didn't ask for a plastic surgeon. The wound, repaired with skin glue, left me with a scar. The bite became swollen, bruised, and infected. I looked like Rocky Balboa for my daughter's third birthday party, and I frightened her and her guests. The bite wasn't my last close call, but it changed my approach to patients thereafter.

RABIES

An awful task often left to the youngest associate in a veterinary practice is processing an animal suspected of rabies exposure. The only way to test for rabies is postmortem, or after death. In my early years as a vet, I worked at three practices affiliated with the local animal control officers. They often brought in dead animals—mainly raccoons—so we could prepare them for testing by removing their heads and submitting them on ice (fresh, but not frozen, for more accurate testing) to the nearest public health laboratory.

At one practice in the suburbs, we had a separate barn structure where I went to chop the heads off the raccoons. For this gruesome task I fashioned "gowns" out of large plastic garbage bags to prevent splatter of blood and other fluids. Often the rabies suspects were already dead, but not always. This meant I had to first euthanize the animal, a task with its own inherent risks. These situations always occurred while I was fully booked with appointments.

One day I was presented with a giant, dead, and entirely revolting opossum already in rigor mortis. I couldn't look at it without screaming, even before I touched it. I covered the body in a tarp, exposing only the head and neck. This enabled me to suppress my gag reflex long enough to disarticulate the head from the body. I howled in horror the entire time. It was the most appalling thing I've ever had to do.

When Things go horribly wrong

My second associate position was in a single doctor practice. I was hired to be the second vet and worked a split shift, with a three-hour break between morning and evening appointments. Since it was located too far from my home for me to travel back and forth, I planned to catch up on work or read in the office during my break. But then I realized the owner saw the break time as an opportunity to nap, shirtless, on the couch in the office. This and other issues helped me decide it was not the right job for me. I found a new job within three months, but put off the time to quit until the very last day to give my two weeks' notice.

That day I worked a Saturday shift alone. The owner lived above the practice and regularly dropped in after appointments to check on the day's progress. This was when I intended for us to have our little chat.

The final pet of the day arrived: a poor kitty who had given birth a few days earlier and was suffering from a postpartum condition known as hypocalcemia. She was extremely weak and lay in a near-death quiet heap on the table. Nursing had depleted her store of calcium and left her muscles weak. This is not uncommon, particularly if the prenatal diet is deficient in nutrients and vitamins. Treatment can be a quick, satisfying fix. Within minutes after an injection of calcium, the mother perks right up. It was a rare opportunity to impress a client and build self-confidence.

The cat weighed about six pounds. Her pet parent insisted on holding her while I administered the injection, along with some replacement fluids to hydrate her. We had a policy: clients were not permitted to assist in pet restraint, as patients could be unpredictable and bite or scratch.

The client persisted. "I'm a pediatric nurse at CHOP (the premier children's hospital a few miles away)," she said indignantly. "I can certainly handle my own cat."

I gave in, partly because she was angry, and her cat was still barely moving, slumped in a recumbent fetal position.

My nurse assistant Jenny had prepared a fluid line for me but was elsewhere doing other tasks. I gave the calcium injection and then stuck the needle under the skin to administer the fluids. This technique is preferred because it saves time and is easier than placing an intravenous catheter. I had done it hundreds of times by myself. But that day, just as the fluids began to flow, the calcium injection took effect. The cat yelped loudly and reached out a foreleg. The cat dug its sharp nails into the client's face, around her eye. The client screamed as her cat dangled by the claws stuck in her face.

As the client howled, I heard a voice I recognized as mine yelling for help. I was terrified of what I might see if the woman's eye was ruptured.

Jenny came in and helped me pry the cat's claw out of the client's flesh. We walked awkwardly, three abreast, up the stairs and then back down to the rear treatment area where I ran cool water onto a rag, placed it over the woman's eye, applied pressure, and tried to summon up the courage to see the extent of the damage.

My heart raced as I envisioned my career running down the drain with the water. Somehow, I managed to quietly instruct the client to remain calm so we could assess the injury. Just then my legs gave out from under me. The top half of my body worked fine, but my lower half was Jell-O. The client stood to my left. My left arm was around her waist, and my right arm held a cold compress on her face. Jenny, to my right, held me upright. I willed my overcooked, noodle-like limbs to cooperate, but they refused.

I finally got up the nerve to look at the eye, which, miraculously, was intact. The cat's extraordinarily sharp nails had entered and then exited back out through the thin layer of eyelid. Two other nails did the same thing below her eye, which spared her from blindness. I insisted she go to an emergency room, and she left, with me still trembling and in tears.

A moment later, my boss walked in. I had no choice but to explain what had happened. He fell over onto the couch and cried. He told me it would have been better, from a legal standpoint, if a client were killed rather than blinded. This made me feel even worse.

I informed him of my plan to leave in two weeks, and he sobbed even harder. He warned me not to call the client, but I ignored him.

I waited forty-eight hours to call. The client told me she had improved, but the wound had gotten much worse before it got better. It was best that I had waited two days to reach out, she said. She didn't sue me.

I never again allowed a client to restrain their cat. I also learned to go with my gut and apologize or admit my role in an unfavorable outcome. Expressing heartfelt concern and acknowledging clients' dissatisfaction can be hard, but it's the only way I have ever known to practice. It's far better to make these admissions to families devastated with loss or things that have gone wrong medically, as families are less likely to become litigious if they sense that their doctor is compassionate and genuinely remorseful.

I worked in over twelve practices throughout my career. Every single first day, I relayed this story to the nurse assistants, horrifying them, but making my point.

I had two weeks to recover from the trauma and drama of that shift, as I was due to start at my new position so soon thereafter. They say that variety is the spice of life. With regard to my patients, things were about to get very spicy for me.

CHAPTER 4

EXOTICS

My third job required me to work with a number of exotic, or unusual, species, in spite of my efforts to avoid them. I inherited many of the previous veterinarian's patients. These included snakes, iguanas and other lizards, birds, rats, and pigs. I preferred a patient attached to a leash, or in a carrier, where I could see them and address them when I was ready. I favored those with legs to the legless, and the winged. But I had a husband to put through medical school, a mortgage, and student loans. So a large number of exotic patients it would be, for quite some time.

When a snake arrived wrapped around an arm or neck, or a rat peeked out of a client's pocket, I ventured out of my comfort zone. It's one thing to take a history and formulate a diagnostic plan while the patient is napping or even growling on the other side of the room. It is entirely different when your patient slithers toward you and you're struggling to move past thoughts of . . . *Does he bite? Is he poisonous? Do you need an antidote for that species' venom?* Necessity proved an effective teacher, and with time I became proficient and almost enjoyed the challenges of working with many of these species. *Almost.*

TURTLES AND THE LIFE AQUATIC

Turtles were never my thing. We had two while I grew up, but my brother was their primary caretaker. In college, a roommate and I had box turtles who shared a small aquarium. They weren't interactive pets. It took me two weeks to realize both turtles weren't just lazy but dead in their tank.

I had a few turtle patients in my career. One had a cracked shell, which we repaired with epoxy. Another suffered from an abscessed leg, requiring weekly antibiotic injections I administered into his shoulder muscles. I pestered him just enough to cause him to stick his neck out in an attempt to bite me, and then I gave the shot in his lower neck muscles. I became adept at treating him without losing any fingers.

My first on-call emergency while working at a veterinary clinic was for an aquatic turtle named Leonardo after a *Teenage Mutant Ninja Turtles* character. His panicked owner was worried Leonardo had almost drowned in his tank and was struggling to breathe. I agreed to meet her at the hospital on a Sunday.

"Where's the patient?" I asked when we were settled in the exam room.

"Right here." She extended her palm to reveal a turtle the size of a silver dollar.

He had gotten stuck between a rock and the wall of his tank and gulped water before he freed himself. Water turtles need to breathe air, and we feared he had aspirated water into his lungs.

Leo was understandably quiet; he'd come close to drowning and spent a harrowing car ride in his owner's pocket, only to be handed off to me, Dr. Clueless, who wasn't yet proficient in turtle treatment.

I did what I would do if he were a dog or cat: I tried to listen to his lungs with my stethoscope, but his body was encased in a soundproof shell the same size as the listening end of the stethoscope. Aware of how ridiculous I looked, I attempted to listen to a chest that was no larger than a casino chip.

The client's sobbing made it practically impossible to hear anything. I rested my hand on her arm and said, "If we're going to help Leo, I need you to be calm."

It worked. He gurgled up some fluid, proving her theory of aspiration.

When she asked about taking X-rays, I said, "Getting X-rays would only stress him more." Translation: I had no idea how to x-ray him and doubted I could see his lungs through his shell. I gave him a prescription for Baytril, the only drug I knew I could use on a turtle, and sent the client home relieved. Leo made a full recovery.

FISH TALES

A few clients asked for advice about their fish. One was a tetra fish who acted abnormally. I reached out to my brother and sister, who each had several tetra fish and knew much more about them than I did. I gave the client some advice, along with a grim prognosis. The fish died as predicted. This was early in my career, when I was learning that it was advisable to give a poor prognosis rather than to promise a cure that might not pan out.

I was a poor fish parent as well. One year, my daughters each won a goldfish at a local carnival. No one wanted to clean the tank, and they were often moved to a back room because of the smell. These fish survived in their filthy tank for two years. I did not have the heart to get rid of them, even while my family begged me to place them in a nearby creek. They would not survive in the wild, having been "pampered" indoor fish.

One day, as my third-grade daughter watched, I switched the fish to a larger tank. I slowly transferred the water and prepared to move the fish. I scooped up one with a net, but she wiggled when I tried to gently grab her. I accidentally snapped her tail and dropped her onto the floor. My daughter screamed as I slipped the fish into the new tank, only to watch her float to the surface on her side, dead. I gave her a quick and solemn toilet-flush funeral. I was much more careful with the second fish and assured my poor daughter that this fish would live. She died the next day. They were the last fish for us.

My son coerced me into adopting an aquatic African dwarf frog from his science class. Scottie turned out to be a very pleasant pet. He swam laps every day, which mesmerized me. I talked to him while I prepped dinner, which I admit was odd. I always found it a comfort to talk to my pets, and a way to get things off my chest. They were such good listeners! Scottie seemed to press his little belly against the glass in response to my chatter. My son soon tired of caring for him, and again, my family tried to convince me Scottie belonged in the nearby creek. I refused, and instead arranged for friends to visit and feed him when we were out of town. Two years later he died at home, from what I believe was old age.

LIZARDS

The list of exotic patients I was asked to treat grew to include lizards—predominantly iguanas. At one practice, I saw them weekly. One "egg-bound" female's eggs got stuck on the way out. Another had kidney failure. He was six feet long, snout to tail tip, and was uncooperative and angry. He snapped his tail at me because he felt threatened. This hurt a lot. Picture me and my assistant trying to flip him over to access the vein on his tail as he snapped at us from both ends.

The rest of the iguanas I treated, approximately fifty patients in all, had one common ailment. Each iguana presented with pathological bone fractures, mainly of the legs, but sometimes of the spine. All were the result of poor nutrition. They had all been purchased at one of two pet stores, where their owners were either given no instructions or poor instructions in husbandry and diet. Feeding lettuce to these omnivores resulted in horribly malnourished iguanas with frail and fragile bones, which appeared like eggshells on radiographs. They particularly lacked calcium, and all needed complete overhauls of their diet, *if* they survived the initial crisis period. It was frustrating because it was a preventable condition. This is one reason why veterinarians are not fans of pet store–purchased pets.

Our practice soon developed quite the reputation for seeing lizards and other reptiles. I saw most patients. My boss mainly came in only to perform surgeries, so refusing to examine iguanas because of inexperience wasn't an option. Because these malnourished patients were ill, they were cooperative. In no time, I inadvertently became Dr. Dawn, Iguana Woman. This was not a lifelong dream realized, but it was my reality.

I saw a few other lizard species, all of whom seemed to have infections of some sort. Time and again I went to my standby medication, Baytril. It was remarkably effective, and I relied on it heavily.

SNAKES

One species I actively avoided was snakes. Yet one day I had a four-foot-long snake come in lethargic and breathing oddly. Before I entered the exam room, I referred to the snake section in my only exotics reference book. Once I determined the snake was nonpoisonous, I needed a clear and detailed medical history for this case.

Today, there is an incredible online resource, VIN, short for Veterinary Information Network, which enables any veterinarian who pays a membership fee to access all the information she might need. This would have made my early career infinitely easier. These days it is invaluable since I work as a single practitioner or do relief shifts without a coworker handy to assist me when I manage complicated cases.

It would have been an enormous help the fifteen years I worked solo as a relief vet. I was working alone one day with a sick ball python snake and a reptile medicine book. I jotted down a list of questions and illnesses the snake might be suffering from. Before I walked into the exam room with my deadpan "I've got this" poker face on, I paused in the hall to say a quick Hail Mary for good measure.

Remarkably, the client replied "yes'" to each of my questions. Her responses grew more enthusiastic with each one. To the unwitting client, it might have seemed like I'd seen snakes every day for years.

The conversation went something like this:

"Has your snake been off of food?"

"Yes."

"Has your snake been hiding in dark corners, breathing rapidly?"

"Yes."

And the pièce de résistance: "Was your snake exposed to a damp area with a sudden decrease in air temperature?"

"Why yes, now that you mention it."

"Was it for fifteen to thirty minutes?"

"Yes. As a matter of fact, it was."

"And did this occur five to seven days ago?"

"Yes! How did you know?"

In my mind, the answer to her last question was either due to the Hail Mary or good luck. I recommended we x-ray the snake, as I suspected she had pneumonia. Did you know snakes could get pneumonia? If I had ever learned it, I had forgotten.

My trusty book got me up to speed. It had pictures of what normal snake lungs looked like on an X-ray, and how they would appear with pneumonia. I played around with the settings on the X-ray machine. The snake "torso" was roughly the thickness of a skinny leg or arm, and I used those measurements as a guideline. It worked. I compared my radiographs to the ones in the book, and bingo! The snake had pneumonia.

How to treat a snake with pneumonia? You guessed it . . . Baytril. I had become the one-trick pony of reptile doctors. I am happy, relieved, and surprised to tell you she made a full recovery.

There is such a thing as beginner's luck. Don't let anyone tell you otherwise.

RATS

I am not a fan of rats. Sorry, rat lovers. I understand they not only make great pets but are the friendliest of all the rodents. I don't dislike them; I am simply not a big fan.

I didn't always feel this way. During my three years of master's degree training, our research involved work with Sprague Dawley rats, a common variety used in lab studies. They were lovely, and I gave them clever names. One group was pasta types—Linguine, Penne, Fettuccine, Orzo. Another was *Godfather* characters and actors—Pacino, De Niro, Brando, Sonny, Michael, Carlo. I became attached to them.

Rats made another appearance several years later in a practice where I did relief work. The regular vet, Dr. Julie, adored rats. Families with pet rats from New Jersey and nearby Pennsylvania came out of the woodwork (pun intended) to see her, and by extension, me, when she was not there.

Dr. Julie dressed in "rat attire." She wore dangling rat earrings to match her rat socks. She displayed her socks prominently, with her scrubs tucked into them mid-shin, held in place with an elastic hair tie. This was around 2005 or 2006, and with her rat-patterned headband, she resembled a cross between Pat Benatar and Jimmy Connors. She could have been a fashion icon in 1985, maybe as an extra in a Madonna video.

Dr. Julie forever ran hours behind in appointments, so we often overlapped during my shifts. She was there to assist with two memorable rat cases of mine.

LUTHER

My first patient was a pet rat named Luther. He was a "fancy rat" (Latin name: *Rattus norvegicus domestica*, for those interested). He was agouti colored—brown, black, and red. Luther had gotten his foot caught in between the edges of a cabinet as he attempted to crawl out, since he enjoyed full access to the home.

When Dr. Julie and I reviewed the hand-developed X-rays together, all I saw were tiny stick figure legs. Had the X-rays been digital, we could have zoomed in by hundredfold magnification to get closer to the details the naked eye couldn't see. But digital X-ray machines were a luxury item most veterinary hospitals didn't have at the time. Many don't today.

Rat expert Dr. Julie nodded with gusto. "Uh-huh. Uh-huh. Yup. We've got ourselves a fracture here."

I couldn't see a darn thing, but I didn't want to appear daft, so I nodded in agreement. I asked guardedly, "Could you point out exactly where it is?" I struggled to see the legs, which were the thickness of a strand of spaghetti, never mind what Dr. Julie insisted was a hairline fracture. Either Dr. Julie was Superman, with vision I was not privy to, or delusional.

"We need to splint this poor baby."

Right. How?

Luther's back leg was two-and-a-half inches long. The fracture was below his knee. We made a splint from half of a Popsicle stick.

Luther dragged his splinted back leg like Quasimodo. I watched, appalled, as Julie bestowed kisses on him with each step. She cooed to him and whispered sweet nothings in his ear, speaking a language only rat lovers spoke. He returned for several bandage change visits, and his leg eventually healed. Personally, I believe he never had a fracture, and if he did, it would have healed on its own, with self-imposed rest. But I've kept my opinion to myself until today.

MARIGOLD

Marigold was a black, Satin variety of rat brought in by a preteen boy who warned us, "Marigold is mean, and she bites."

But Dr. Julie knew better. She explained she was a "rat whisperer." We brought Marigold back into the treatment area down the hallway from the exam room and clipped and cleaned her wound. She bit my index finger, as I was the designated assistant. I then watched in horror as Dr. Julie administered oral antibiotics to Marigold—one drop followed by a full kiss on the mouth, another drop, another kiss.

Dr. Julie whispered, "How much do I love you, my little Marigold?" She planted more smooches on the disinterested rat.

We entered the exam room, and Dr. Julie demonstrated her amorous technique of drug administration to the clients. Marigold had endured one kiss too many. She latched onto Julie's upper lip and dangled there until we could pry her loose. Blood dripped from Dr. Julie's shocked face as she handed Marigold back to the little boy.

He looked at her with an incredulous expression. "Why would you kiss her?" he asked. "I told you she was mean."

BIRDS

I have a love-hate relationship with birds. I grew up with a myna bird, but that did not endow me with ease in handling the large parrots and macaws I later saw at three hospitals I worked in. The first was a clinic where I volunteered for two summers while still in veterinary school. About a third of the patients were birds. We did everything from routine medicine to cardiac workups and full blood work.

A beautiful scarlet macaw named Eliza lived at the facility. She calmly perched in the office and was free to fly around at will. Eliza hated me and randomly attacked me. At first, we thought it was because I wore red, but wearing other colors didn't help. Next, we speculated that my large head of dark hair set her off. Ponytails and baseball caps did not make the problem go away. I tried to always be the one to feed her, in hopes she would develop a fondness for me as her provider. She preferred lunging at my hands to breakfast and dinner.

Eventually, we traced her motivation to attack me to a time when she'd witnessed me restraining a parrot who needed a cardiac workup, which involved connecting him to electrode clamps that transmitted his heart rhythms to a cardiology facility. The parrot squawked in distress while Eliza watched, appalled. Apparently, she'd held a vendetta toward me ever since. Plus, we were forced to confine her for my shifts, which made her despise me even more.

A few years later, I saw many bird patients at the same practice where I treated all the iguanas. Not long after working at that practice, I did relief work in a different hospital, also with a large number of bird patients. They were impressed that my résumé included reptilian and avian experience, which had me concerned I would soon be known as Dr. Dawn, Bird Doctor. I was still not yet in a financial position to turn down shift work, since Dave was a medical resident making close to peanuts, and we had two babies toddling around.

While I can't say I was an expert in avian medicine, I became much more proficient in handling birds and their medical needs.

I learned to take any symptoms of illness seriously enough to deal with them sooner rather than later. Birds are fragile creatures who can go medically downhill in an instant. Any bird issue is considered an emergency. Even the stress of a beak or nail trim can kill them.

One client, Genevieve Minsky, took a liking to me largely because her bird Cindy, a hyacinth macaw, seemed calm and happy to see me when I trimmed her beak and nails. Cindy did not easily take to strangers, nor to immediate members of the Minsky family. She also did not like men. Her receptiveness to my handling was a first for me, and I felt relief and a bit of pride now that I was finally the object of a bird's affection.

Soon after Cindy became a regular for these "spa" visits, Genevieve got it in her head that I might be a good choice as the bird's caretaker in the event of Genevieve's death. Larger parrots, known as psittacines, can live for decades. Hyacinth macaws like Cindy, the large cobalt-blue birds, have a potential life span of fifty years. African greys, cockatoos, conures, cockatiels, and parakeets all have varied and often quite long life spans too. Because some outlive their pet parents, it is not unusual for veterinarians to be named in wills as designated caretakers should the clients pass away. (I discuss pet trusts in more detail in Chapter 13.) While flattered, I was not prepared to be the potential beneficiary of a pet that could live as long as me. Plus, the odds were pretty good that Cindy wouldn't like my husband.

I saw bird patients rarely throughout the rest of my career, but they were not out of my life completely. My sister Faith has had several conures—small parrots, diverse in size and color, with the ability to speak. Conures are referred to as the "clowns" of the parrot world, known to have attention-seeking behaviors, and hers exhibited those characteristics to no end.

Faith worked at a bird clinic in southeast Florida, so I called her and her staff if I had an avian question I was unable to answer myself. The only problem was that whenever I tried to phone, her two birds, Pecker and Petey, were so jealous of me diverting her attention away from them that they would loudly squawk and yell profanities at me in the background. I could barely hear Faith above the ruckus.

To entertain them while Faith was at work, my mother "bird-sat" them at her home. She taught them to speak with language CDs and played music throughout the day. They picked up phrases quickly. They also memorized the lyrics of parts of several songs by Frank Sinatra, Perry Como, and The Four Seasons. Petey's rendition of "Walk Like a Man" was spot-on in pitch and bore an uncanny resemblance to Frankie Valli's.

PIGS

My limited experiences with pigs is notable. When my teenage daughter wanted to adopt a "teacup" pig, I told her absolutely not, explaining that these cute pigs start off miniature but soon become enormous. I had heard many tales of pigs being abandoned once full-grown because people were confused about what they were buying, or because sellers misrepresented which breed was being sold and left their customers with unreasonable expectations.

Here are the facts: Teacup pigs (also referred to as baby tea-cup, mini teacup, micro-mini, dwarf, and pygmy pigs) are the same species as Vietnamese potbellied pigs, originally bred in Vietnam. They can grow to between one hundred and one hundred seventy-five pounds. There are several variations, both in size and temperament, which make some better adapted for living indoors than others.

While working at a practice in the semi-rural suburbs of Philadelphia, I saw a few pigs for basic medical care. This included annual teeth trimming, hoof trims, parasite control, and vaccines—mainly leptospirosis, tetanus, distemper, and rabies. These pets lived indoors and outdoors. Clients liked to send photos of themselves with their pet, who was often named Wilbur, lounging on the couch.

While they are known to be very clean and intelligent, pigs intended to mainly live indoors do not fare so well. They require adequate space, are "opportunistic scavengers," and spend a lot of time rooting around in search of food. If kept indoors, they can be destructive; instead of digging in the ground, they turn their attention to new carpeting or expensive furniture.

Lack of mental stimulation can lead to boredom and then aggression toward humans. Pigs living alone in a home do poorly behaviorally because they are social animals. Sadly, they often end up being transferred to sanctuaries after families find they cannot cohabitate with them.

There were other reasons I did not wish to adopt a pig. For one, I had enough trouble finding dog sitters for my dog, India. Imagine the effort it would take to find a pig sitter. I didn't know of any kennels that took in pigs.

Two other significant events caused me to shy away from taking on pigs as pets. The first occurred in veterinary school, at the large-animal campus where I famously lost Taz the Thoroughbred. While there, I assisted in a pig surgery to de-scent a one-hundred-fifty-pound potbellied pig. Potbellies have two scent glands—thin-walled sacs of noxious fluid. The odor from these glands is one of many reasons these pets are often abandoned. (The retention rate is an appalling 5 percent.)

A classmate and I were in a surgical suite, a large unheated, barnlike structure. I was dressed in layers, including a wool sweater worn under my scrubs.

At one point in the procedure, the surgeon accidentally nicked one of the sacs. The odor was so terrible I lost my sense of smell for several days.

After surgery, I wrapped the soiled, offensive sweater in a plastic garbage bag, tied it tightly, and forgot about it for six months. When I finally took it to the dry cleaner and opened the bag, the stench of boar hit me so strongly it felt like a slap in the face. Off to the dump the sweater went.

The second event happened while I was the only doctor present for a hospital shift. I received a frantic call from someone in Northeast Philadelphia living in a row house with a bleeding 250-pound pig named Willie (short for Wilbur, no surprise). The pig had gotten his hoof caught in a door, and a sharp piece of metal trim sliced into his skin. They were located forty-five minutes away and heard we treated pigs, as we did see the occasional potbellied pig for vaccines. But these pigs were brought in to see us. This person expected me to come to her home to collect the bleeding pig, who could be heard squealing at high decibels along with the client. I encouraged her to seek help to transport Willie. She managed to arrive in a neighbor's pickup truck. I stemmed the bleeding, now only a slow trickle. Willie's cracked nail healed within the week, but it took several days for me to regain my full ability to hear.

Ironically, I would soon discover that I was in the perfect position to help clients with bleeding pigs in their homes.

CHAPTER 5

HOUSE CALLS

That desperate pig in Philadelphia may have planted a seed in my mind, because I decided to start my own house-call practice not long after. After years of relief work, I missed following up with patient progress, and I was tired of being rushed out of exam rooms when clients needed more time to understand their pets' conditions. In particular, I enjoyed working with senior clients and thought I could make a difference seeing them in their homes. I was disheartened whenever I met elderly pet owners who lived alone and depended upon taxis to transport them and their pets to see me at clinics.

I finally decided to open a mobile practice after performing a handful of home euthanasias. I had previously assumed clients would forever link the place where the procedure was performed with the memory of their pet dying, so I was initially reluctant to do it in their living room, kitchen, or bedroom. As it turns out, euthanizing in the pet's comforting environment was the ultimate gift of love, and the only way I would ever consider saying goodbye to my own pets thereafter. After all, we have memories of our pets throughout the home. It is also much easier on the families. More details follow in Chapter 16.

In pet parents' homes I found my true calling, rising to multiple challenges, all in front of my clients. There were dermatological puzzles to solve and medical mysteries to diagnose and treat. I didn't have a backup doctor to run a case by, or to help me collect blood from a tricky vein. On any given day I might be asked to treat a new puppy or kitten, and on the next visit, asked to end a life humanely.

Sometimes when I entered a home the patient was hidden under a bed or a couch, or in an attic. I became part doctor, part detective as I sniffed out clues as to where the patient was hiding, hoping in the process they had not become extra excited or aggressive, or that their medical condition was worsening as I hunted for them.

Many families request a house-call vet because their dogs are giant, older, and arthritic— Great Danes, mastiffs, Bernese mountain dogs, Newfoundlands, Anatolian shepherds, Great Pyrenees, black Russian terriers, and Leonbergers. What is a black Russian terrier or a Leonberger, you might ask? I had never seen one of either breed until a few years ago, and then I saw many. Often each family had several. One family had two mastiffs, each weighing two hundred pounds. It's hard to load a car with one, never mind two, or even five, of these dogs.

Most house-call patients needed to be seen at home because they were too fearful, or even feared, in the hospital setting. Behavioral issues are the most common reason for skipping visits to the clinic. This is precisely the type of patient who needed a vet like me. Many of my canine patients didn't get along well with other dogs. These pets had to enter the veterinary hospital through the back entrance, or only after the front waiting room was cleared of other patients. They were generally sweet, wonderful dogs when I saw them individually. But with each other or other pets, not so much. They were far more at ease on their home turf.

For the relatively small number of patients I had as a single practitioner, a fair number of them were on prescription behavior medications. Most had generalized anxiety. Many also had separation anxiety. Some had noise phobias. Several had a combination.

The majority were unhappy without their medications, and a potential risk to family, friends, and neighbors if they acted aggressively out of fear or anxiety. Behavioral consultations could be time-consuming, but it was very rewarding when I helped a family and a pet remain together.

I also saw many cats with anxiety who developed inappropriate urination habits, a top reason for pet relinquishment or euthanasia. The literature now refers to it as inappropriate toileting, which includes defecation outside of the litter box. Anxiety and aggression in dogs, and inappropriate urination in cats, are the most common reasons for turnover to shelters.

Not all pets can be helped by medical therapy alone. In fact, I only recommend medication for behavioral issues when it's used in conjunction with behavioral therapy. Trainers, veterinary behavioral specialists, and clients working in tandem can help many animals and truly save their lives. With time and hard work, I have been a happy witness to these pets becoming affectionate, trusting members of their families.

SEBASTIAN

For nearly twenty years, my friend Aimee and her family have adopted abandoned dogs with medical issues. One dog was missing an eye, another was blind in one eye due to an injury, and a third had three legs. They brought home senior dogs who sat in shelters for months, because older pets are difficult to place with families. Two years ago, they adopted a La Paz, a mixed-breed dog with a severe autoimmune skin disease. She was essentially bald when they brought her home. She required ten different medications and treatments daily, and has seen both me and a dermatologist on a monthly basis.

And then there's Sebastian. Before she found him, I hoped Aimee's next dog would be a healthy puppy, free of disease. Someone with whom my friend would enjoy a long life. Instead, Aimee rescued Sebastian, who was found by the side of the road and left for dead after he was hit by a car. His left hind leg was shattered and he spent close to a year at a veterinary hospital, where he endured twelve surgeries to save the leg. He was left with two toes instead of four and was unable to bear full weight on the leg. Essentially, he was three-legged. He fit right in with Aimee's other rescue dog, Annie, whose left hind leg had been surgically removed after she was shot.

Understandably, Sebastian's experience left him with a severe case of white coat syndrome (the fear of doctors' white coats and the smells, pain, and unpleasantness that can come along with them). I met Sebastian at a clinic where I unfortunately chose to wear a white coat to work. He was terrified and lunged at me aggressively. We had to muzzle and sedate him, then and prior to subsequent visits. But we were not about to give up on him.

Sebastian developed a severe case of separation anxiety when Aimee left him unattended at home. He clawed through a wall and a door twice. He produced puddles of drool, broke out of his crate once, and injured himself.

Aimee and I devised a treatment plan to help Sebastian understand that she would soon return after an absence. She left him for progressively longer periods of time, and several months later, he improved enough to be left at a lovely kennel where he was allowed to sit alongside the receptionist at the front desk all day while he boarded.

Sebastian never needed anxiety medication, and the turnaround in his demeanor was remarkable. He became my first house-call patient six months after his adoption. When I arrived the first time, he barked loudly, stormed into the glass door, and then bounced off of it. I wondered how we would manage the exam, but once I came in, he lay down and relaxed as Aimee petted his head. He licked me continuously.

Since that day, I am greeted with the same crazy barks, after which he rolls over and demands a belly rub. Few patients have ever brought me the joy Sebastian has, and fewer actually like me as much as he does. He is one of the rare pets who is not afraid of me.

The advantage of a home visit is that a calm, familiar house helps to ease the anxiety of an exam. It is even more important for nervous patients. In an effort to help the exam go smoothly, I confirm appointments ahead of these house calls and often give explicit instructions so the pet parents and the pet are together in a room awaiting our visit. Despite the prompting, many clients are often not only unprepared for our arrival but also involved in a project I deem inappropriate or inconducive to a house-call exam. They might be painting their house when we arrive, or roofers are banging and hammering above our heads while I attempt to listen to a pet's heart. Music commonly blares, or a television is playing so loudly I am forced to request they turn it off. (I am amazed at the popularity and longevity of *The Price Is Right*. I am convinced there may be a 24/7 channel devoted to it.) The opposite of the Zen mood I strive for is a roomful of children playing Fortnite and yelling at the screen.

MAYBE WE NEED A DRESS CODE

Fortunately, in the house-call milieu, the pets are generally more at ease than in the hospital, and the client is as well. The same pet owner I have seen in the hospital for years may present as a completely different version of themselves in their home. I arrive ready to see the neatly dressed, seemingly organized, calm, and patient person I met in the hospital, but instead I'm greeted by someone wearing pajamas, mid-conference call, and yelling at whoever is unfortunately on the receiving end. While my assistant and I set up our supplies, the pet owners will eventually walk in and act as if we hadn't heard any of their conversation. It's also not unusual for us to arrive in the middle of an argument between the pet owner and their spouse or children. A common misperception is that we cannot hear them from the kitchen, where they left us with the puppy or kitten. But we can.

I understand that people can forget to complete their outfit prior to our arrival if they are, say, in the middle of a work call when we get there. That doesn't explain why two clients felt compelled to strip down and show me the bite wounds they sustained as they broke up a fight between their dogs. Their terriers often scuffled with each other or other dogs. They even avoided trips to animal hospitals for fear their dogs would fight with other pets in the reception area.

That day we were dispatched to evaluate the wound on one of the dog's back legs and determine if it could be treated without stitches. It could. The owner's injury to the inner thigh could not. He pulled down his pants, showed me the bite, and begged me to fix it. His wife's ankle bite was smaller. Mercifully, less of a burlesque show was required for me to view her wound. Clients rarely want to make a trip to the ER, report a bite from their own dog, pay for a doctor visit, and waste time in an office or hospital. I refused to treat their wounds and got out of there as fast as I could.

During our post-visit chat, I blurted to my nurse assistant Natalie, "Aren't you glad his bite wasn't on his butt?"

CATS (AKA IT'S THE VET, HIDE!)

As a house-call veterinarian, I encounter many cats, most of whom hate the veterinary office. Cats stress easily. If you take them out of their routine, they sometimes revolt. If you change their litter or diet or have too many or too few people in the home, it can cause them anxiety. That anxiety can make them act out inappropriately and can cause disease.

We now understand how to better coexist with cats and enrich their home environment to reduce stressors. There are a multitude of triggers that can cause unease, and I ask specific questions to unearth why cats fight with each other in the home, act aggressively toward the owner, or frequently get sick.

Helpful information might include whether there is the correct number of litter boxes for the number of cats, the type of litter, and how frequently it is changed. Feeding is important too—how often and how much food is offered, the distance between the wall and the food bowl, and the feeding location in the home. If cats with a perch or windows exposing them to birds, other cats, or people experience that as a stressor, I need to be made aware of it.

It is not unusual for cats to vanish at the time of their house-call exams. Many clients theorize the cats overhear our phone conversations while the visit is scheduled and plot to make themselves scarce the day of the appointment.

Cats also have short intervals of patience for their veterinary exams. The only way to get the upper hand is to be quick and efficient as I examine, vaccinate, or collect lab samples for testing. If we spend an hour corralling the patient, we lose the stress-free advantage of a home visit.

I ask pet parents to lure their cats into a powder room or bathroom a short while before I am due to arrive and to leave them there. It is a controlled environment without beds to hide under and closets to get lost in. It seems like a fairly easy instruction to follow, right? The doctor asks you to confine the patient, so you confine the patient. Yet a surprising number of clients insist the cat remain in the wide-open family room, where he or she always enjoys greeting visitors.

"Oh, she's the friendliest cat you'll ever meet!"

"That's silly! She loves everyone!"

And the most common, "Yes, I got your instructions, but I decided not to keep her in the bathroom. She'll be just fine."

In my experience, the client who protests the most has the rare patient we cannot catch, and we have to give up the chase and "call it." This has happened only five times. I have pulled my aging back out on several occasions lifting furniture in search of cats. And I still needed to charge for the visit because a forty-five-minute cat hunt takes the same time, if not more, than what's allotted for a full exam and visit. It makes for an awkward moment and is best avoided.

I was once desperate to finish a double cat exam after I spent half an hour catching the first patient. I had the second cat, a nineteen-pound Maine coon, grasped in my two hands while I was face down and splayed out under a four-poster bed. The client and my assistant Natalie dragged me out by my feet. Now a human Swiffer, I emerged fully covered in dust. Natalie and I needed Benadryl and a shower after the appointment because we both experienced full-blown dust allergy attacks.

It is a wonderful day when the feline patient is pleasantly amenable to our exam. More often, this occurs on a first-time home visit. At our return trips, most cats recognize our scent and even seem to know the sound of my car's engine as I pull into the driveway, so second visits are rarely as smooth as the first.

BRUTUS

Brutus had a terrible reputation for becoming highly stressed whenever he needed to go to the vet hospital. His parents dreaded those visits. Perusing his previous veterinary records, I noted they were full of red dots, warnings, and notes about his "screaming in exams, which could be heard throughout the hospital and frightened waiting rooms full of patients." It was an alarming document to read.

The owner, Mrs. Theroux, fully admitted she was apprehensive the visit would end in failure. She asked if I had the thick, long leather gloves other veterinarians had used to manhandle Brutus. I had a pair. I had only used them twice to collect a rabies suspect from a trap for testing. I never used them in the home.

Brutus weighed twenty-nine pounds. Imagine three average-sized cats rolled into one giant, screaming, snarling, scratching agent of terror awaiting our arrival. He was not confined to the small downstairs half bathroom as suggested. He sat on the landing upstairs, where he preferred to hang out.

Mrs. Theroux explained, "Being locked in the bathroom will just aggravate him and get him in a worse mood."

That day we planned to see both Brutus and Vidalia, his much smaller, friendlier sister. She was lounging along the top of the sofa when we arrived. We examined her first and had trouble with her from the onset. The client was perplexed, as Vidalia was known as the more well-behaved member of the duo. It occurred to me she may have confused the cats.

With all our fingers intact, we apprehensively headed upstairs to deal with Brutus. There, leaning on the railing, was arguably the largest cat I had ever seen. We approached him with our typical overfriendly, high-pitched, yet just-above-a-whisper greetings. Brutus just sat there, his legs splayed out in front of him, and . . . did absolutely nothing.

We took our thick towels and cradled him in them. He quietly cooperated. We thought it wise to transfer him to a bathroom and did so without event. He also needed vaccines and a blood and urine collection for an intermittent issue his veterinarians had, for years, failed to successfully test for and treat. Brutus did not show a single bit of resistance, not even a growl for good measure.

When I now describe Brutus, I refer to him as a mellow ball

of fur. We have a scale of aggressive/difficult-to-work-with cats, which ranges from 1 to 10. Brutus was a 1 or -1. Vidalia was a 3. Mrs. Theroux was incredulous, doubtful we had examined Brutus because of the lack of the ear-splitting screams she was accustomed to hearing.

TMI

Because people are at ease on their home turf, they tend to chat more readily. Perhaps because we frequently end up in client bedrooms, trying to coax nervous dogs, and especially cats, out from under beds. This intimate environment can open the door for sharing—or, some might argue, oversharing. One cat who was MIA at our arrival was Melvin. He was hiding under a laundry pile in the master bedroom. He was a serious flight risk and very strong as he fought us throughout the exam and collection of blood.

My assistant Natalie and I were absorbed in our work when the client began to discuss some new bras she had purchased. She described them as "wonderful" and "life-changing."

Natalie and I glanced up and noticed myriad bras in various shades of magenta, electric teal, and white, hung to air-dry throughout the room. Immersed in the exam, we'd missed visual clues to give us a context for the off-topic conversation. The bras were so huge and there were so many that I presumed their awkward presence prompted the client to explain them.

Just as Melvin was about to bite us, the client lifted her shirt to show us just how comfortable and fabulously formfitting the bras were.

I mumbled something like, "That's great," or "Ooh, pretty!" and wrapped up our visit.

A quick Google search confirmed the client worked as a sort of "Avon lady" for bras. Trapped with her cat, we'd been subjected to quite the informal product pitch indeed. The home-sales spiel is not unusual. Countless clients have offered us samples of face serums, jewelry they make, artwork they sell, legal representation, and offers to barter.

Guns A-Blazing!

Bras aren't the only weird things I've seen during home visits. I've entered many homes while clients have had guns out, in the process of being cleaned, loaded, taken apart, or still warm after they just returned from target practice in the yard. It's not only strange to me why someone would do this just prior to having their puppy examined but also cause for alarm when I enter with my young female assistant. Who knew my pre-exam prep should include "Please have your guns put away"?

One client, Gwen, ignored my standard advice to sequester her four cats to a small room, preferably one without clutter and furniture where cats could hide. Instead, the cats were dispersed around the home and the hunt was on. We corralled three of the four in the master bedroom. Armed with thick towels, Natalie, Gwen, and I called out the cats' names. We heard movement. Then boxes and shoes came crashing to the floor as the cats attempted to flee the room. One kitty, weighing about fifteen pounds, slammed into the door at eye level. He sprung up several feet midair, then rebounded off the ceiling and disappeared under the bed.

I dreaded lifting king-size mattresses and frames since I'd pulled my back out twice previously doing so. I positioned myself at the head of the bed and instructed Natalie and Gwen to lift the bed while I planned to swoop in and somehow grab the enormous—and now frantic—patient.

I noticed a gun under the mattress, lying atop the bed frame. I was near the gun, and the cat was six inches away as Gwen and Natalie held the mattress up over their heads.

"Gee. There's a gun here," I said.

Gwen responded, "What gun? I don't have a gun."

I replied, "Yes, you do. It's right here, under where you place your head every night."

Gwen and I argued about the gun's existence for a while, then had a battle of wills over who would remove it from under the bed.

"You grab it!" I said to Gwen.

"No, *you* grab it, you're closer," she insisted.

I ignored Natalie's glare as she begged, "Don't do it. Don't touch that gun!"

I desperately wanted to catch that kitty. Against all reason and judgment, I moved the gun to a shelf and treated cat number one. As I did, I asked, "Is the gun loaded?"

Gwen replied, "How would I know? I didn't even know I had a gun!"

In the search for more patients, I spotted an open box of bullets atop a dresser. This was also a surprise to Gwen. We captured and treated three of the four cats. I briefly worried that I would be contacted by the police, dusted for fingerprints, and linked to a suspicious shooting, but thankfully it never came to pass.

MARGARET AND HANK

Homes come in all forms. Many of my mobile clients lived in nursing homes or assisted living facilities. Margaret was one such wonderful client who lived with her cat, Hank. The only way Margaret's daughter Donna was able to convince Margaret to move into an assisted living facility was on the condition that she could take Hank. I agreed to make the forty-five-minute trek each way for home visits.

Margaret was hard of hearing. She also had selective hearing. She overfed Hank and denied that I instructed her to feed him less. She conveniently lost the papers where I wrote down the exact amount of food Hank should eat each day.

Over time, as Margaret stubbornly refused to skip his daily scoop of vanilla ice cream, I watched Hank get heavier and heavier. Every visit and weigh-in documented a slow, progressive march toward diabetes. I dreaded the thought of treating Hank as a diabetic—what the frequent visits required to manage his disease would mean for me as his doctor. To prevent such an outcome, Donna and I conspired to change Hank's diet. To my relief, after two years his weight leveled off.

Every visit, Margaret forgot to leave Hank in the bathroom in her apartment. On one visit I rooted around for him in the closet, and on another under the large, heavy bed. On my most recent visit he cleverly hid "in plain sight" in the center of the bed, under the blankets.

Margaret wasn't just stubborn and hard of hearing; her memory was deteriorating. I was particularly alarmed one day when I greeted her in the lobby and she didn't recognize me. I was signing in on the visitor's log as she told me and the receptionist that she was there to wait for Hank's veterinarian. I had to explain to Margaret three times that I was the vet.

The next time I saw Donna, I gently expressed my concern. Worrying about Margaret's dementia kept me up at night. Not long after, Margaret fell and hit her head. She remained on the floor of her bathroom for over twenty-four hours before she was discovered.

When Margaret was transferred to a medical unit, Hank needed a new home. It's challenging to place older cats in rescue groups, as they often come with medical issues and there are costs associated with extra veterinary care. Coincidentally, that week an acquaintance named Nora reached out, asking if I knew of any cats in need of adoption. Nora wasn't put off by Hank's age, and she had no other cats in the home, which was necessary, since Hank did not do well living with other cats. Donna's family provided funds to help with the transition and veterinary fees.

Hank would be welcomed by Oscar, a sweet black Lab just waiting to cuddle Hank when Hank was ready. Still, this would be a logistical nightmare. Poor Hank was stressed over strangers coming in daily to feed him, and bereft from Margaret's sudden absence.

We hatched an elaborate plan for transferring Hank. I arranged for a sedative to be given prior to our arrival to help us get him in a carrier. A trial run did not go well, as he refused the food we mixed with the drug. We eventually medicated him by grinding up the drug and sprinkling it on Hank's favorite treat—vanilla ice cream.

My house call crew and I met up with Donna and her brother Mike at the assisted living facility, and our team was able to get Hank into the carrier. I took him to my house, where he met his new mom, Nora.

After several weeks, Hank not only acclimated to his new home, he ruled the roost. He took over Oscar's spot on the sofa, and the patient Labrador sweetly allowed Hank to groom his ears.

Margaret sustained memory loss with the fall, but after several conversations about Hank, she finally absorbed that he was gone from her life and in a good home. While their separation was sad, we were pleased we had avoided the likely alternative—that Hank would have been placed in a shelter and not adopted; ultimately, he probably would have been euthanized.

DOING WHAT I DO BEST

The house-call environment was at times daunting, since I worked in unfamiliar spaces under the watchful eye of the clients. But it forced me to hone certain medical skills with no margin for error. There were no associates on hand to offer second opinions, and it was imperative to establish a professional demeanor and to communicate effectively with clients so they understood when and why further tests were needed to help make a diagnosis.

I'm innately well suited for explaining complicated medical conditions in layman's terms. Colleagues have asked me to assist as a consultant for this purpose. I first try to put a family or owner at ease enough to trust me, and then I guide them toward the best decision for their pet. This is easier to do on their home turf. Reading a client's mood, emotions, and way of processing information, which can be complex, is key to helping them understand. Some clients are detail oriented and want to know medical minutiae, while others prefer I share the big picture without any specifics. Some respond to a hug for support, while others prefer distance and verbal support.

Many pet parents are not comfortable with a watch-and-wait approach; in order to move forward with a treatment plan, they need answers in the form of biopsies or every test imaginable. Others trust in my empirical judgment of their pet's likely diagnosis.

Often I need to assess the client within the first few seconds of a conversation, as this initial chat sets the tone for all future interactions. I have become proficient at this and no longer get complaints of being too technical, not technical enough, talking down to a client, or being deaf to a client's wishes or financial constraints. My rewards are long-term relationships with phenomenal clients who entrust me with caring for their beloved pets for the animals' lifetimes. It's a privilege few physicians enjoy, given the specialization of human medicine. I consider myself blessed in this regard.

I also have three more true gifts, or talents, two of which have proved invaluable in house calls. One is extracting the very last bits of urine from the world's largest obese cats with the smallest bladders, using a urine-collection technique known as cystocentesis. I am better at this than anyone I have ever met.

One assistant, after working with me on house calls for just a few weeks, commented, "Damn. You are pretty kick-ass." She muttered this under her breath, because the client of the fat, hissing cat in question was with us in the powder room while I obtained the "liquid gold" with an extraordinarily long needle.

Extra points to me for instructing the client, "Look away if you've ever fainted, because this looks worse than it is." I say this because three clients just about dropped to the floor when I performed this procedure on their pets. And we all know how sensitive I am to the issue of clients fainting during my exams.

At another home visit, a different assistant told the client, "I'm not sure you realize how incredible it is that Dr. Filos performs this procedure successfully without the aid of ultrasound to find the bladder!"

It's less a talent and more of a magic trick I learned from a veterinary nurse, coupled with some medical and anatomical background knowledge. It's my claim to fame, at least within my small veterinary circle.

My next bit of expertise is an acquired skill. When I worked in a veterinary hospital, I brought patients to the back of the hospital's treatment area, away from clients, to collect blood or place intravenous catheters as needed. These procedures can be a bit daunting to perform in the hypervigilant presence of a pet owner. But I have now been in hundreds of people's homes to euthanize their elderly, ill, and dying pets. This requires me to access the smallest, most frail veins imaginable. Sitting with the distraught family just inches away, in their pet's final moments, is not the time to struggle with a vein. I have become remarkably good at it.

Finally, while not imperative to house calls, I have an uncanny knack for visually estimating the number of pills I need to count out for a patient. Veterinarians wear several hats, often acting as their own pharmacists, so this trick comes in handy often. If I need, say, 120 thyroid pills, I will pour out a mound with the exact number, give or take a tablet. This, too, is only a source of entertainment for the niche veterinary clinic environment, and would not garner applause on *America's Got Talent*. Sadly, I cannot do the converse and guess the number of jelly beans in a jar. I have yet to win a prize in any such contest.

BOB AND ELAINE (AND ZAC)

I credit house calls with supplying me with some of my most profound and gratifying professional experiences. One recent visit highlights what I do best. My clients Bob and Elaine lived with a small terrier mix named Prozac, Zac for short. He'd been given a quirky name because he was an anxious dog adopted by an anxious owner. Zac was lethargic, had trouble swallowing, and made odd noises that sounded similar to the benign reverse sneezes most dogs experience. When I learned they'd been occurring several times a day for two weeks, I planned a house call.

As with all nervous pets, I quietly entered the room, sat on the floor, and chatted with the owners, ignoring Zac. He came over to me a few minutes later, straddled my lap and discovered the hidden dog treats in my pocket. I noted that he chewed on the left side only, and I quickly pried open his jaw to find a very loose, diseased tooth and a mouth full of tartar-laden teeth, which explained his abnormal jaw movements and lack of appetite. When I suggested a cleaning and removal of the loose tooth, I sensed Elaine's reluctance and immediately phoned the practice I work in conjunction with for anesthetic procedures. We scheduled it for the next day.

Good news, I thought. But Elaine began to sob. She hugged me, and then left the room.

Bob said, "Wow. Thank you. Do you have any idea what you just did?"

To me it was probably the simplest case I would see all day. Not a diagnostic challenge, and an easy enough fix.

Bob went on, "We've been chasing Zac around the house

for two weeks, trying to look in his mouth. Elaine hasn't slept well the entire time, and Google searches convinced her Zac was dying of cancer. She held off calling you, afraid of bad news. He doesn't trust anyone. The fact that he let you examine him so easily was miraculous. It's as if he knew you would help him. And you knew Elaine needed you to be the one to schedule the dental procedure." Bob patted my hand and offered a heartfelt smile. "You're not just an incredible vet; you're an intuitive people person. That's what makes you so special to us."

It was the greatest compliment I could ever receive. I've never underestimated the stress a sick pet can have on the entire family. It's proof of just how emotional and deep our attachment is to our pets. The love that pet parents show their pets is expressed in profound ways. I've seen it time and again and have been inspired to share some of the stories of my amazing pet families in the next chapter.

CHAPTER 6

THE THINGS
WE DO FOR LOVE

I 've noticed that animal lovers can't seem to get enough movies, books, and television channels devoted to pets. It makes sense. After all, living with and pampering their pets leads people to search for more resources to teach them how to do it even better. They need to know things, like why pets sniff or groom each other, and whether or not they dream. Do they see color? Are they lonely if they sleep in their crate at night, or do they prefer it?

One thing they know for sure—their pets love them unconditionally. As a post-COVID society, we all desire this bond now more than ever.

PET SERVICES

As numbers of no-kill shelters rise, more people are rescuing pets, especially when adoption fees are next to nothing compared to the escalating costs of purebreds. My mother lost a bidding war on a Maltese breeder's Facebook page to another person willing to pay $2,000 more than she was. Add to that the fees for a service known as "flight nannies," who chaperone puppies from around the globe, should the United States fall short in supply of your desired breed.

There has been an explosion of services available to satisfy the desire to spoil, pamper, or show love for animals. And an explosion of spending—some dog parks have membership fees rivaling my gym. In cities such as Philadelphia and New York, real estate costs are higher the closer you get to dog parks.

I help out a posh dog kennel that has a bone-shaped swim-therapy pet pool with multicolored lights. Clients pay extra for their pets to do laps while their parents are out of town. They have indoor and outdoor play groups, heated beds, and televisions in most rooms. When I visit, I wonder who's had the better vacation: the family or the dogs. (In all honesty, if I died and came back as a suburban Labrador retriever or a cat with one of those fancy self-cleaning litter boxes and exercise wheels costing upward of $700, I would be okay with it.)

Should you prefer to bring your pet with you on vacation, there are transport airlines for pets. One such company, VistaJet, has a VistaPet division, developed with veterinary consultants. The flights are equipped with groomers and dietitians, providing meals such as prime beef or fresh fish, along with herbal-infused water. Flight attendants offer massages, and are trained in all aspects of first aid. They also offer a four-week period of desensitization to manage in-flight stressors such as the sound of jet engines, loss of cabin pressure, and turbulence.

I have a client who paints dogs. I don't mean that she is an artist painting pet portraits. She actually paints the dogs themselves, to resemble little foxes, raccoons, or rainbows. She dyes them to match a bridal color palette, and they stand alongside bridesmaids or function as ring bearers. She makes good money for this service. So do stylists for the dog-and-cat-show circuits. I have an acquaintance who pays her mobile groomer $350 per visit.

I refer clients to trainers, some of whom host dogs in their homes for immersive behavior programs. A few weeks and several thousand dollars later, they are returned "cured" and with instructions for maintenance. One family I know adopted a puppy who arrived both behavior- and potty-trained.

Not all advances in pet training are frivolous. I know of families who have created GoFundMe campaigns to raise money to train and purchase service animals. One adopted a miniature schnauzer named Sheila for their daughter who suffers from epilepsy. Sheila alerts the family if she senses the child is about to have a seizure. Guide dogs trained to help with vision loss and other physical disabilities, as well as emotional support pets, are invaluable to many lives. I have seen trauma-assistance-trained dogs accompany rape victims into court to face their attackers.

Of course, some people falsely claim their pets are service animals, to the detriment of those who legitimately rely on trained dogs to function. News stories abound about people's attempts to convince flight attendants that their peacock or cockatoo, for example, are emotional support animals. I understand the desire—we want our pets with us—but doctors and therapists are better judges of genuine need than airline personnel.

Thankfully, much more often I work with people who truly amaze me with their willingness to treat and make sacrifices for their pets. Some will cancel a vacation to pay for their dog's unplanned knee surgery. Others will end relationships—if the cat has urinated on the man's shoes one too many times, out goes the man! I manage patients whose daily drug and supplement schedule is so complicated I wonder how the client is able to hold down a job and make time to administer the frequent dosings.

Pet families truly inspire me. The amount of money they're willing to spend on their pets is a small fraction of what they are willing to do for them. The emotional commitment and sacrifice is what truly defines pet parenting. Pets may be defined, by law, as property, but in reality they are seen and treated as beloved members of the family.

I have been inspired by the devotion to pets I've witnessed for decades. I am sometimes taken aback by the lengths my clients will go to for their sick dogs or behaviorally challenged cats. I've happily provided support to some extraordinary families committed to providing a better life for the animals they adopted, often after others had given up on them.

At the same time, it is important for those of us who work in the veterinary profession not to have unreasonable expectations of pet parents. This is especially crucial when a family is forced to make the difficult decision to sign over a pet to their veterinarian, a rescue group, or a shelter to be adopted into a new home. This may be due to financial constraints or lifestyles that don't allow them to adequately care for a chronically ill pet in need of long-term medical treatments, such as diabetic cats, dogs with Addison's disease, and pets with destructive separation anxiety requiring management and medication. Moving forward with treating such pets requires a commitment of time and money a family may not have to give. It can be a severe hardship on those who travel for work or are already caretakers for other family members.

Compassion fatigue is real. If we determine the burden to properly care for a pet is excessive for the family, we sometimes collectively make the hard decision to either rehome the patient or to euthanize. Veterinary professionals should base their advice on the best outcome for the pet. This requires carefully listening to clients to ensure the family completely understands what is required to properly manage the pet's care. It is crucial that they have realistic expectations. The process takes time, and sometimes difficult choices must be made.

Sometimes the decision is euthanasia to spare the patient from prolonged suffering. I have watched clients make this hard choice based on love for their pet, guided by their wish to ultimately give him or her a better life. It's rare that a client will ask me to arrange for the adoption of an elderly pet with manageable yet incurable issues, because we know how difficult it is to place old pets. Finally, when animals pass away, more pet owners choose to have pet funerals now as well.

MELLY

An inordinate percentage of my patients have anxiety about vet visits. The unpleasantness of traveling in a pet carrier and car compounds what may already be a harrowing ordeal for most patients. Pets prefer routine, and only a small number enjoy the visit to a veterinary hospital. Most endure it, and some need sedatives or muzzles and reel from the experience for days.

Melly, a mixed-breed dog, was adopted from a shelter three years ago. We estimated her age as close to two. She was shy when her family met her, but the two elementary school–aged children fell in love with her. While she eventually warmed up to the family, she cowered when strangers and the children's classmates visited. This worsened with time.

When I visited, Melly was tense and nervous. She crouched in a ball, with her tail tip close to touching her nose. We needed to unravel her contorted little body to help her stand on all four feet.

Her parents were reluctant when I suggested antianxiety medication in conjunction with behavioral modification training. This is not unusual. The stigma of "puppy Prozac" is a common hurdle. We made some progress with training, but at each home visit I discovered a new trigger that sent Melly into an emotional tailspin. Thunder, fireworks, other dogs, doorbells, and extended time spent by herself made Melly tremble and skip meals. She eventually suffered what I believed was a seizure. After that, her parents agreed to try Prozac.

Melly had a minimal initial response and her appetite decreased, which is a common but usually temporary side effect of Prozac. From the onset, I had recommended the parents meet with a veterinary behavior specialist, but the costs and distance were deterrents. Instead, they worked with a trainer with whom, after several months, they felt comfortable leaving Melly for a week while they vacationed.

When they returned, Melly looked terrible. She had lost weight, developed diarrhea, and reverted to her previous anxious behavior. The setback was the impetus they needed to meet with the specialist, who instructed them to increase the Prozac dosage.

Melly improved in small, slow increments. Then she tore a ligament in her rear leg and required extensive orthopedic surgery. Poor Melly relapsed behaviorally as a result. She worsened further when the surgery had to be repeated. Several months of rehabilitation and many thousands of dollars later, Melly growled and lunged at mail carriers, children on their way to the bus, and other dogs, all of which passed by her home several times daily. Neighbors knew of Melly and warned me to "avoid the scary dog around the corner."

The family was afraid to leave the house for extended periods of time. They were reluctant to kennel Melly, and attempts to find a dog sitter failed given her unpredictable aggression. Desperate, the family found a kennel with day care facilities where they left Melly for a week while they vacationed. They returned to an emaciated Melly, who refused to eat, had diarrhea, and was lethargic.

It was heartbreaking to see Melly worsen. I ran blood work, which came back normal, and treated her physical symptoms. But the anxiety medication regimen wasn't working. The specialist, unusually, did not respond to our calls and emails. I decreased the Prozac to twice daily. I hoped the drop in Melly's appetite was from both the medicine and stress. I added Xanax because it often helped my other patients get extra anxiety relief. Most of my patients took it at night to help them sleep through storms, early morning garbage truck noise, or other stressors. I had not had huge successful turnarounds in the past but prayed for any positive response for poor, dear Melly. Miraculously, Melly improved within a week. Each day brought progress.

Recently, while on a walk with my dog India, I saw a dog approaching us. As the dog and its owner neared me, I was shocked to realize the happy, tail-wagging, friendly dog was Melly. She rolled onto her back and demanded I give her a belly rub! She and India became instant buddies. I was elated. Melly's transformation was more extraordinary than I could have ever imagined. Xanax freed her of the shackles of anxiety and unearthed the happy, lovely girl we always hoped and believed was there.

GEORGE FREEMAN, JRE, ELASTICAT, AND JUMBO

My mobile practice has brought several disabled and elderly clients into my life and my heart, including George Freeman, a self-described "crazy cat man." He is not to be confused with the boxer George Foreman, who he mentions more or less every visit. George is one of the kindest, gentlest, most generous people I have ever met. He was one of my first clients, and I have loved and worried about him for years now.

George lives by himself in a trailer development. He suffers from several injuries that have left him partially disabled. He collects toys, coins, and electronics, all of which he loves to show us. He's placed several heated cat houses throughout his neighborhood and offers smorgasbords of cat food everywhere. I schedule extra time for his visits since he always wants to chat. I leave each house call feeling sad and wishing I could have spent the entire day there. I hate to leave George on his own.

Originally, George had two cats, JRE and Elasticat. Later, he adopted Jumbo, his son's cat. I learned that JRE was a cartoon reference to Jerry, of *Tom and Jerry*, and not Jerry Garcia (my first guess). Elasticat is tall, long, wiggly, and aptly named. He often escapes our hands, towels, and grip.

Jumbo, now known as Super-Jumbo, weighed in at twenty-nine pounds after a year in his new home. George would do anything for the cats except put them on a diet. His kitchen resembled a pet food mini-mart, with a buffet selection of dry and canned foods. George insists the cats are finicky, but you would never know it by their weights. All three steadily got heavier each visit, and George chuckled when I gave him the "It's not a question of *if* but *when* they will become diabetic" lecture.

I leave most visits frustrated after George tells me, "Aw, Doc, how can I deprive them of food when they love it so much?" At last check-in, I am happy to report the cats were doing well. Their weight was steady and none were diabetic.

George is generous to a fault, and not just with his cats. I leave time for his surprise requests to examine a neighbor's cat or two. When one of his friends walks in at the end of a visit or George guides me to their home, I find it impossible to say no to him. I watch as they argue and he insists on paying their bill, which further delays the visit.

Those same neighbors helped me twice when I arrived and George did not open the door. In the past I had gone to the window and rapped loudly to wake him. A few times I became concerned, seeing George's car but no George. I enlisted his neighbor, a one-time client of mine, to use his spare key to check on George.

I always expect the unexpected when I visit George, and I wouldn't have it any other way.

ELVIS

I have worked with many families from all walks of life and varied tax brackets. There is no way to predict what a client is able or willing to sacrifice for their pet, regardless of whether they can easily afford a treatment or surgery. It is my job to offer them options and guide them to the best decision for them and the patient.

When a client is forced to decline services that are too expensive, it's difficult for me and the family. If young children happen to be in the room at the time, it is even worse. One Christmas Eve, I worked a busy shift at a cat clinic, where I met Caroline Shreve and her young sons, Carl and Matthew. They brought in their Himalayan cat, Elvis, who had gotten out the night before and returned with a severe limp. I suspected he had been hit by a car and had a broken hip and back leg.

Elvis was wonderfully cooperative, given the amount of pain he must have been in. Carl and Matthew, around eight and ten years old, sobbed when I suggested Elvis had a broken bone. Matthew mentioned how he had suffered a dislocated shoulder after a collision on the soccer field. The boys were about my son's age at the time, and their sweet, empathetic faces melted my heart.

I explained that X-rays were necessary to determine the extent of the damage, but I was optimistic and hoped the injuries were limited to the bones, with no internal bleeding or other complications.

Caroline called me aside and confided that her husband had just been laid off work. She was reluctant to move forward with the X-rays. She hoped cage rest and inactivity would heal Elvis. I doubted rest would be enough. She agreed to the radiographs, which would tell us just how bad his injuries were and guide us to make a well-informed decision.

Unfortunately, Elvis had a dislocated hip and a mid-thigh

fracture. While the hip could be relocated and bandaged with sedation, the combination of it and the fracture made surgery the only viable and humane option.

Caroline spoke with her husband. He did not want to move forward with any treatment. Surgery wasn't an option financially. The boys were devastated and begged me and Caroline to fix poor Elvis. She called her husband back, and we both tried to convince him to allow us to formulate a payment plan for the procedure.

Then the boys got on the phone and begged him. "Let her fix Elvis! He's so sad. Take back all our Christmas presents. Please. We don't want anything. We just want him to be better."

Their father agreed to a payment plan and discount. By now, several nurses, the receptionist, and the other doctor there that day had fallen in love with Elvis and the boys. We each donated to the Shreves. I insisted our boss meet the family, and he offered them a generous holiday discount to do the surgery. Elvis stayed in the hospital for three days. He was a star patient, and his progress made my holiday.

HALO

I met Halo, a border collie mix—part Labrador, part border collie, part something else—when she was already somewhat senior. She was a stubborn, medically high-maintenance girl, and I needed to see her far more often than a young dog. For that reason, and the fact that she was amazingly resilient, lovely, and tolerant of me while trembling when I walked in the door, I fell in love with her.

Her family was extraordinary. They did anything and everything possible to keep her comfortable and pain-free. Halo had severe arthritis, particularly in her front limbs. Her front legs were curved when I met her, due to the remodeling of her painful joints. This worsened with time, prompting me to recommend specialists and numerous tests to make sure she had nothing other than arthritis, such as an immune-mediated disease like lupus, or rheumatoid arthritis. Expensive tests ruled out those diseases. Still, her elbows worsened. The cocktail of pain medications, injections of joint supplements, and CBD helped, until they didn't.

Halo was the first patient I helped make $1,000 custom orthotics for. We were so excited when they came a month later from Canada via FedEx. We strapped them onto her legs, and . . . SHE REFUSED TO WEAR THEM. I felt so guilty and heartbroken, but her parents said, "Well, we gave it a shot." That was it. I was essentially a geriatric specialist at this point, and I had exhausted every resource for Halo. We had gotten her comfortable, and agreed to disagree about trying to acclimate her to the dreaded orthotics.

Several months later, Halo suddenly stopped eating and became anemic. Other blood work and an abdominal ultrasound were normal. New specialists concluded that one of her medications, a non-steroidal anti-inflammatory drug that had never caused any stomach upset before, was now causing intestinal inflammation and ulcerations. We scaled back on the drugs we had so cleverly combined to keep her comfortable.

Ultimately, the calls and quality of life consultations came more frequently. While I should have seen this coming, I was accustomed to Halo rallying, as she had so many times. She had more lives in her than any cat I have ever met. Mind you, this is a dog who was walking around on front legs that defied gravity well before I even came into the picture. I was devastated when we scheduled her euthanasia. My assistant Carreen, who saw her regularly for nail trimmings at their home, was equally wrecked to hear the news.

We made a plan, scheduled a date, and prepared emotionally, only to receive a call that Halo had rallied yet again. We'd scrap the plan, tweak medications and doses, and she'd surprise us with her determined will to march on. This went on until one day early in the COVID-19 isolation period, when I got a desperate call and texts, stating that it was the dreaded day to euthanize Halo.

Throughout the morning and afternoon, it was sunny and warm. All my patients were cooperative, and no muzzles were necessary. It was a rare day when all went as planned, and proved to be too good to be true. We arrived at Halo's at the end of our appointments and met her pet parents on the porch. Halo had a wonderful last day. She ate like a pig the day before. I was relieved to see her leave on a high note, instead of being ill and lethargic. It was all settled and resolved in my mind. I knew it was the right thing to do.

And yet, after I gave her the sedative and I returned to assess if she was ready for us to progress, I lost it. Halo was audibly dreaming. She was snoring. She was sedated, and yet was still so alive and so much like my own dog at home, whose loud snoring forced me to raise the volume of the TV. Halo was hardly gray at all, I noticed. She was peacefully asleep and her mom was sobbing, leaning over her head. I, too, was distraught and had trouble seeing through my tears as I began giving the final injection. I realized later that day, while logging in my controlled drug journal, that Halo was the 185th home euthanasia performed since I started my house-call practice. I had been through this 184 times before. I was good at detaching. But I wasn't good at it that day. I was sweating in latex gloves and a mask. I sobbed and couldn't wipe my eyes. My nose ran into my mask, and I couldn't blow my nose. My clients were sad, and I couldn't hug them because of COVID-19. It sucked. I always hug my clients. There was no way for me to express my sympathy to them directly. Instead, I hugged and then kissed Halo, through the mask at first. Then I pulled it back and gave her a tiny, direct kiss. I said goodbye, because she would remain at home and be buried there. Some patients snag my heart. Halo did just that.

MODERN LOVE

One last story highlights a perk of my job: being privy to wonderful, heartwarming, life- affirming stories about pets. People always want to talk about their dogs and cats, horses . . . you name it. If I am at a party or somewhere where I know no one, all I have to do is mention what I do and invariably, I make an immediate connection.

This next tale is a personal favorite. Recalling it always gives me an instant mood boost. I had a client named Bethany, whose dog Churro was the Chihuahuan equivalent of a Walmart greeter in Bethany's retirement community. He was regarded as the unofficial mayor and was accustomed to six walks a day, rain or shine, as he did the rounds and visited with his neighbors.

When Bethany needed back surgery, she arranged for Churro to stay with a friend for the several weeks of her convalescence. He would share the friend's home with three Labrador retrievers and two cats, and get regular exercise of a different sort.

Bethany's friend let Churro sleep next to her in bed during his stay, since he was missing his mom. She fell in love with him and soon began to dread his return home. It prompted her to adopt another small dog of her own to fill the void left by Churro's departure. Enter Hermione the cockapoo.

Not only did Hermione find herself in a new loving home, but she also found herself a . . . husband! She and Churro were instantly smitten with each other. Bethany informed me that the two dogs were officially "engaged," and that I was invited to the wedding. Theirs was to be an unconventional, modern arrangement where the bride and groom would reside in separate homes and visit each other several times a week.

I was consulted about where to find yummy party favors that picky Churro might enjoy. I referred Bethany to a fancy pet bakery nearby. The nuptials were a lovely outdoor affair, black tie optional.

There is real joy in being a veterinarian. Churro and Bethany brought me joy, as did many others in my career. There is also much humor in the situations that present themselves when pet parents, particularly new or inexperienced ones, are faced with uncertainty, when their pets act sick, or make odd noises. Sometimes the hardest part of my job isn't explaining to clients what's going on with their pets but keeping a straight face while doing so. Pet parents can be quite entertaining without meaning to be, as you'll see even more clearly in the next chapter.

CHAPTER 7

PET PARENTS DO THE DARNDEST THINGS

Veterinary medicine is anything but mundane. I've often wished I had a GoPro camera strapped to my forehead to capture the uniqueness of my profession. Just when I think I've heard or seen it all, I'm enlightened and amused by animal-related news or surprised by something a client does or says. Client reenactments of their pets' maladies are arguably my favorite part of the workday: coughing, hacking, growling, hissing, snoring. I doubt I'll ever retire, because life without pet lovers and their exploits would be far less interesting.

IMITATION IS THE SINCEREST FORM OF FLATTERY

I went to the home of first-time pet parents to check on their cat, Licorice. While she waited in the powder room, I had them describe the behavior and noises that worried and confused them. The husband crouched in the corner and hissed loudly. His wife corrected him and showed me her impersonation of Licorice's high-pitched yowl. For extra drama, she scratched at her husband with her arm and fingers extended, just like Licorice had. Both complained about how Licorice occasionally even bit their ankles. They asked if Licorice was ill or perhaps in pain.

Licorice ate well and was physically normal. She was showing her anger with growls and swatting and aggressive play behavior that had been going unchecked for months. While the behavior itself wasn't humorous, the clients' complete lack of cat savvy surprised me.

We determined Licorice's aggression was prompted by their unsolicited cuddles. I found the couple's behavior endearing yet misguided. Once they learned to respect Licorice's space, they all enjoyed a happy, healthy relationship with each other.

REVERSE SNEEZES

The most common nonemergency "emergency" acted out by countless clients is the reverse sneeze. It can be alarming to watch your dog snort histrionically. Many clients worry their dog may faint or has something lodged in his or her throat. Before I give my rendition of a reverse sneeze, I ask clients to show me what their dog does. They do their best to snort and gasp. I then convince them it is rarely anything to worry about.

You may be familiar with this behavior if you have lived with dogs. The first time it happens, it is understandably scary. Paroxysmal respiration, commonly known as a reverse sneeze, occurs when a dog rapidly pulls air into their nose. With a regular sneeze, the air is rapidly pushed out through the nose, hence the name. The loud noise is a result of an attempt to inhale at the same time as a sneeze. It is not a harmful condition, and there are no ill effects. If you have seen your dog do this and he or she was completely normal before and after it occurred, it was probably a reverse sneeze.

While the exact catalyst is unknown, any irritant in the nose, sinuses, or back of the throat can trigger an episode. These irritants might be nasal mites, secretions such as saliva, foreign bodies like seeds, pollens, grasses or other allergens, or smoke. Less often, the culprits might be masses or extra-long soft palates, which are typical of certain breeds, or sometimes narrow nasal passages, which are common in dogs with long noses.

If the behavior occurs frequently, your veterinarian may suggest tests or radiographs to rule out a tracheal or heart condition. Occasionally, anti-inflammatory medication will be prescribed. Try to remain calm and ease your dog's anxiety to curtail the episode.

REGURGITATION VS. VOMITING

The distinction between regurgitation and vomiting is an important one and a key clue to differentiating one set of problems from another. In these instances, I am the one called on to mimic the pet behavior. Regurgitation is more of a passive behavior and results in the upchuck of food. It's an "Oops, my food just came up" moment. Vomiting is a more active physical process, with muscles recruited and sound effects employed. Neither scenario is humorous, but my rendition of regurgitation vs. vomiting is pretty entertaining. If there were an Academy Award category for "Best Impersonation of Animal Behavior," I could be a contender.

SCOOTING

My version of scooting would get honorable mention . . . maybe. I prefer to have clients demonstrate how their dog drags its rump around.

Dogs and cats have anal glands, or anal sacs, situated at three and nine o'clock at the end of the rectum. They produce an excretion with a scent intended to notify other animals of their sex and health status and to mark their territory. Normally these glands empty during a bowel movement. If that bowel movement is soft, or if something else is awry, excess secretions can build up, impacting or infecting the glands. In an attempt to relieve the discomfort, animals will rub or lick at the area or drag their bottoms (scoot) across floors and furniture.

Dogs are especially prone to this problem. While some cases are associated with seasonal or food allergies, others may present after a bout of diarrhea. Some dogs will try to empty their glands when stressed, while others simply need more fiber in their diet.

Cats experience it as well, but they are more subtle about revealing that they are ill or uncomfortable. I get the occasional client call describing a teriyaki-colored smear on their linens. Or the "dead fish odor" from their cat's mouth, deemed "much worse than the normal dead fish odor" that manifests after they actually eat dead fish. Cat parents more often report that their pet pays an excessive amount of groom time and attention to their hind end. Or they are extra grumpy, or cry when they defecate in the litter box.

I am often called to empty the glands and fix the problem. On occasion, clients ask me to teach them how to empty the glands themselves. I do my darndest to dissuade them and emphasize, "There is no situation I can think of to prompt me to do this by myself at home. Please, allow me to do this for you today and in the future."

If I fail to successfully impart this message, I send them off with a recommendation for a large bottle of Vaseline and gloves, detailed instructions, and my heartfelt blessings.

IT'S ALL ABOUT THE CALORIES

An alarming percentage of pets are overweight. Much of my day is spent advising clients how to help their pets lose weight. These conversations can be contentious, because of course it's the pet parents who need to change their behavior, since the animals aren't feeding themselves. I try to be diplomatic, but I don't always succeed—a boss once chastised me for telling a client, "Your dog's not exactly able to drive himself to McDonald's."

Many pet parents show love with treats and food, and this is a hot topic in many households. I have refereed many arguments between spouses as each accused the other of overfeeding the cat or dog. Or they blame the grandmother, the children, anyone but themselves. It's no wonder that the higher the number of people in a home, the greater chance the pet will be overweight or obese.

Several years ago, there was a medication available to decrease dogs' appetites. I refused to dispense it until all other attempts at weight loss failed. In my mind, it bordered on unethical for me to prescribe a drug for the dog when client behavior was the underlying cause of the issue. Increased exercise and less food made sense, in the short and long term. Yet I was repeatedly shocked by clients who preferred to medicate their dogs instead of feeding them less.

Home visits give me a distinct advantage regarding diets and portion control. It is not enough to write down amounts and calories. My weapon against the war on obesity comes in the form of one key request I now make in my home visits: "Show me the cup."

Not everyone agrees on how much a cup is. A Pyrex measuring cup clearly shows that it holds eight ounces. But people choose different size cups for feeding their pets.

Jeff and Evelyn were the pet parents of Jenny, a yellow Labrador retriever who was close to thirty pounds overweight. All prior diet attempts had failed. When I started my house-call practice, they were among my first clients. As our conversation circled back to Jenny's weight problem, Jeff banged his fist on the table and yelled at Evelyn.

"Show her the cup!"

Reluctantly, Evelyn brought out a plastic Big Gulp cup from 7-Eleven. This "cup" was more like six cups. Thereafter, I instituted a show-me-the-cup policy with overweight patients.

Sometimes there isn't even a cup. Many clients also use automatic food dispensers, which, while convenient, are problematic if the pet is motivated by food, boredom, or a combination of both.

Other times the culprits are outside the cup, in the form of treats or "rewards" that are simply not considered as part of the pet's daily calorie intake. Take Flora, for example. Flora was a cocker spaniel who suffered from severe ear infections in both ears. I showed her mom, Kathy, how to clean the ears and then apply the medication and told her to do so morning and night for two weeks.

I returned for a recheck and weighed Flora before I examined her ears. I was surprised to see she had gained five pounds in the three weeks since our last visit. For a twenty-five-pound dog, a five-pound weight gain is significant, and I chalked it up to scale error. While she felt plumper to me, I didn't push the issue. I needed to see her ears.

We placed Flora on a table, and she was uncharacteristically cooperative for her exam. She allowed me to extend her left ear and look deep into the long canal to see her eardrum. It was uncanny how she turned her head ninety degrees and bent over so I could take a closer look. Each time she flipped her head, I heard a strange "swoosh" sound. I was focused on the ear but eventually asked Kathy, "Did you hear that? There is it again. Sounds like 'whirrush.'"

Eventually, I noticed that each time Flora flipped her head over, Kathy squirted a dollop of Cheez Whiz onto the table. Flora happily lapped it up while I probed her ears. This had been going on for two weeks. No wonder she gained five pounds! We had fixed one problem and caused another.

OOPS, I DID IT AGAIN...AND AGAIN...AND AGAIN

Certain pet procedures are best left to professionals. I have previously cautioned against emptying your dog's anal glands at home, for example. Not only is it messy and smelly, but there is a risk of doing it wrong and causing injury to the spine and exacerbating inflammation. Infected anal glands are often indistinguishable from impacted glands, and we might miss an opportunity to treat an abscessed gland before it quite literally explodes into a larger problem.

Clients are sometimes surprised that I refer them to professionals for their pet's grooming as well. Proper grooming requires training and experience. I understand that clippers are readily available online and in pet stores, and I sympathize with the desire to do it yourself to save money, time, and a stressful visit to a groomer. But not all pets will sit still for an extended period of time, and wiggling pets are at greater risk of injuries. Groomers understand the importance of adequate restraint, know where and when to cut, and are cognizant of how close they are to the skin, which can be alarmingly close to knots and mats.

I speak from experience. When I adopted my mixed breed, India, I made several attempts at trimming her. I have given haircuts to friends and family members for decades, and many are repeat customers. How hard could dog grooming be?

It's not as easy as you might think. I made a mess—my home and my body were covered in dog hair. India became less cooperative with each successive session and emerged with an asymmetrical coif—she looked like a client of Edward Scissorhands, in a bad way. She seemed embarrassed to be seen in public after I hedge-trimmed her natty coat.

Clients also regularly take it upon themselves to give their dogs and cats haircuts, against my advice. One family stands out in my mind, as I was asked to treat the fallout from haircuts gone awry.

The Burgess family had several pets: three Himalayan cats, a standard poodle, two Labradoodles, and a shih tzu. These are probably four of the most popular breeds, and they are all on the top-ten list for high grooming needs. I had grown quite fond of them all over many years of visits to keep their four-legged brood in good health. I understood the family's desire to save money and groom their pets themselves, but they ended up paying significantly more in veterinary fees.

The first inadvertent injury was when they sheared off Happy the cat's nipple with clippers while attempting to remove her mats. I stemmed the bleeding with blood-clotting medication, applied pressure to the wound, and removed her other mats without bloodshed.

Happy returned a year later with an inch-long laceration from scissors they used to cut another mat on her inner thigh. I begged them to take her to a groomer for regular shaves because she was an overweight long-haired cat and not as limber as she needed to be to adequately self-groom the hard-to-reach areas on her belly and near her rump. Happy was not at all happy, and neither was I.

Theo and Vinnie, the Labradoodles, made it their mission to get into trouble. They swam in the pool several times a day during the summer and tracked water and mud throughout the house. Not a summer month went by without a trip to their home to treat an ear infection. The combination of summer seasonal allergies, heat, and moisture created a ripe environment for infection to thrive. Both dogs had hairy ear canal openings, which made it harder to air out and dry the ears to prevent future problems.

One day the Burgesses got busy with those dreaded clippers on both dogs' ears, nicked the skin, and called me in a panic. I arrived to find a bloody kitchen reminiscent of a horror film set. Vinnie had been cut and reacted to the pain by shaking his head obsessively, spraying blood all over the walls and ceiling.

Veterinary hospitals have permanent bloodstains on the ceiling for this reason, but it is far worse when it happens in a client's tastefully decorated home. In lieu of repainting, I wondered if it would be cheaper to accessorize with a Jackson Pollock or two.

As if this wasn't enough of a reason to get rid of those darn clippers, they called me out again to see poor Hillary, their standard poodle. She had knocked over a bottle of maple syrup. The evidence suggested she'd rolled in it, because it was all over her back, feet, and face. She became a walking adhesive, trapping rocks, sticks, and gum in between and under her toes. The offensive clippers sliced through the large foot pad, which is quite vascular and necessary for a dog to bear weight. There was no easy way to suture this fragile tissue. I cleaned the wound, carefully cut out the gum, used a surgical skin glue to reconnect the damaged wound edges, and bandaged her. I insisted they surrender those troublesome clippers once and for all and refused to leave until they handed them over.

As much as I enjoyed seeing the Burgesses, I preferred it to be for routine health checks. If you find yourself in the clipper aisle at PetSmart, I beg you . . . just walk away.

WOULD YOU MIND REPEATING THE QUESTION?

Clients don't just *do* the darndest things, they often say them too. Some silly comments I have heard include the following:

"No, I don't need flea products. She's an inside dog that only goes outside to use the bathroom."

"Do her kidneys sound okay?"

"Every time my dog kisses me on my mouth, I get cold sores. How can I get it to stop happening?"

"My dog isn't overweight. She has heavy muscles, so she weighs more."

"He's not in any pain. He just limps."

"I think my dog got cancer because he always sleeps too close to the router."

"I burp my puppy after every meal, just like a baby, because she is a baby."

"I've decided not to spay her because she's a purebred pit bull/husky/boxer mix."

"We can't possibly do the X-rays today. They cost as much as six manicures."

"I realize she's spayed, but we've decided we want to breed her anyway."

While I see the humor in these comments, I understand that for the most part they come from a place of genuine love and concern for their pets' welfare. Someone distraught about their pet is oblivious when he says his dog is "sick as a dog." Clients will go to great lengths to assist by giving me a thorough medical history. If it involves a demonstration of how their pet acts, I am all for it.

CATNIP

The combination of cats and catnip always makes for an unusual day at work. Soon after I opened my mobile practice, I advertised at outdoor fall harvest fairs where I raffled off baskets. One client was the lucky winner of a cat-themed gift basket containing bags of catnip, among other items. He left the basket open on the porch for his two cats, Mr. Wrinkles and Chubby, and then went out for several hours.

I received a concerned phone call from him several hours later. He had arrived home to find Mr. Wrinkles and Chubby passed out on the patio atop a mess of cellophane, cat treats, and toys.

I mentally pieced together what had happened. The cats, who were allowed to roam the property during the day, had come upon the basket. They maniacally ripped into the catnip and scarfed down several bags of Temptations and Fancy Feast treats as well. It was a classic case of a catnip-induced, extended cat nap.

MARIJUANA, AKA THE PEOPLE'S CATNIP

A better title for this subsection would be "Clients Who Lie." Until recently, marijuana was not legal in most states, and clients or their teenage children were reluctant to admit that their pets had been exposed to pot. It made my job harder. Not only are my patients unable to speak for themselves, but if they act out of sorts or seem off and I don't get the full story, I am at a further disadvantage.

I learned early in my career that most, if not all, of my patients exposed to marijuana have a telltale symptom: they dribble urine. Dogs and cats who "act funny" and urinate around the house is the reliable tip-off I need. They may also seem uncoordinated or wobbly on their feet, drool, vomit, or have dilated pupils. High doses, while extremely rare, can cause serious neurological symptoms such as tremors or seizures.

Most conversations go like this:

Me: "Mrs. Smith, does anyone have marijuana in the home?"

Client: "No. Of course not."

Me: "Do you have any teenage or college-age children who might have some?"

Client: "No. Not my Jimmy. He's a straight A student."

Me: "One of his friends, maybe?"

We continue until I explain how I will need to run a quick urine test screen (not accurate in pets), and if negative, will need to do more tests that are more expensive and must be sent out to a special lab. If this doesn't work, I say, "You realize I'm here to treat Fluffy, and I'm not required to report any suspicion of use of illegal substances to the authorities." This usually prompts a confession.

If there is a teenager present, staring at their feet, I make an excuse to leave the exam room and loiter as I wait for the teen to step out to "use the restroom." This is when they admit just how much weed "went missing," and I ascertain whether there was chocolate involved. Pot brownies are more of a concern because the theobromine, methylxanthine, and caffeine levels in the chocolate can be toxic depending on the amount ingested. Treatment must be tailored to the dose ingested and the severity of symptoms. Generally, concern over the safety of the patient overrides the awkwardness of the situation. I am lucky to have been spared many seriously ill, overdosed patients in the course of my career.

INEXPERIENCED PET PARENTS

New pet parents sometimes blurt out the funniest things. One lovely young client named Kevin brought in his Norwich terrier puppy, Luigi. Kevin rattled off the usual questions about how to choose diet brands, amount of food to give, and how to train Luigi. Then he asked how often he needed to bathe Luigi. I explained how some breeds need to be groomed and require more frequent baths. Then I mentioned that my Labrador only got bathed when he was extra dirty.

Kevin said, "How many times a day or a week should I bathe him?"

"Pardon?" I wasn't sure I'd heard him correctly.

Kevin looked sheepish. "I bring Luigi into the shower with me every day. I thought he needed a bath every day, like people."

I bit back a smile. "And he's okay with this?"

Kevin shook his head. "I think he's a little tired of it, honestly."

Yes, I imagine Luigi was tired of his daily baths! I formed a picture in my mind of the puppy wearing a bib and seated in a high chair, being spoon-fed his food. I chuckled at the thought.

MISTAKEN IDENTITY

Another family had just adopted their first puppy. They were told he was a Chinese crested dog. I am sure they paid a fair amount of money for the puppy, but I am also convinced it wasn't a Chinese crested. The breed has two varieties. One is hairless and only has small tufts of hair on the head (crests), paws (socks), and tail (plume). Sometimes they have a beard. The other variety is the powderpuff. It looks completely different, with a long, soft coat of varied colors.

What neither variety has is the tightly wound curls of a poodle, which is what this dog had.

The clients were told the curly hair would soon fall out and never grow back. They asked me when they could expect that to happen. I told them never. They had so much faith in their breeder, I was forced to pull out books with pictures of all variants of the Chinese crested breed to prove my point.

I am often amazed at the extent to which clients will believe a "breeder" and take their advice over mine. It took a while, but I convinced them they had been bamboozled and had purchased a sweet miniature poodle. They were a bit "crestfallen" at the news (pun intended).

OVERZEALOUS PET PARENTS

I once saw a couple with a boxer named Ophelia. While the husband grew up with dogs, this was the wife's first time as a pet parent. She was determined to be the best dog mom ever, and she bathed Ophelia and brushed the dog's teeth regularly. She also thoroughly palpated Ophelia's body once a month.

I was asked to the home that day to check two cysts the wife had noticed in the dog's vagina. She explained that she regularly felt for tumors, having been warned that boxers are prone to cancer. While I appreciated her intent, I was taken aback. This level of pet care was unusual. Evidently my mouth dropped open in shock at such a revelation.

Her husband was surprised too. He gaped at her and asked, "Why would you even do that, and then tell the vet?" I felt bad for the woman. She was trying her best, and I tried to smooth over the awkwardness in the room as best I could. I commended her on Ophelia's lovely teeth and coat and assured them self-administered pet exams were not necessary with regular veterinary care. I think I convinced them both, but for good measure I blurted out, "Heck, I spend half my day with my hand up dogs' butts." We all nervously giggled and moved on.

Another inquisitive family had a list of questions about their new Saint Bernard puppy, Lexie. She was a good sport and allowed the three children and their parents and me to handle her and listen to her heart with my stethoscope. The children each used the ophthalmoscope to peek into her eyes, and the otoscope to check her ears. Lexie endured not one but four exams that day.

Toward the end of the visit, the dad said to his middle school–aged daughter, "Come look at Lexie's vulva. It's here in the back of her mouth. It looks different from ours."

Hmmm. I think he meant *uvula*, and I subtly corrected him. Lexie was in good hands with this charming family doing their best to care for her.

Delicate situations like this merely skim the surface of my career, which has been laden with awkward moments, as you will read about in Chapter 8.

CHAPTER 8

THAT WAS AWKWARD

People and pets can be unpredictable and funny. There have been many times during an exam when somebody did or said something awkward.

On the last day of clinics before I graduated from vet school, we were treated to a show featuring a stand-up comedian/veterinarian. He shared hilarious stories from his career, and he inspired me. Of the hundred-plus students in our graduating class, several of my classmates went on to admirable achievements—they worked treating famous racehorses, as head vets at theme parks and aquariums, or in academia. Yet the possibility of one day being a veterinary comedian enthralled me. My job soon proved full of opportunities to amass humorous material.

During exams, patients are often less than cooperative. While it wasn't ideal, if we were short-staffed in the clinic, we sometimes allowed pet parents to help hold and calm their wiggly dogs. As discussed already, apprehensive cats defensively bit and scratched, and I did not let clients hold them. But I made exceptions for squirmy puppies.

I once inadvertently grabbed a male client's crotch as we struggled to restrain his fidgety dog. One minute I was busy palpating the dog's abdomen, and next thing I knew, I was palpating the owner.

I DIDN'T CATCH YOUR NAME

A very pregnant client came in with her dog and two children. She shared that she was expecting a girl, whom she planned to name Tiger Lily. I thought she was kidding.

"Ha ha. No, really," I said, "what are you actually naming your baby?"

"Tiger Lily," she repeated.

Digging an even bigger hole, I asked, "So, are you calling her Lily for short then?"

"No, we'll call her Tiger Lily," she said.

Mortified, I stammered, "Of course! How nice." I stared at my feet.

Moments later, she yelled, "Peter, Nana, stop fighting! Tinker Bell needs her shots."

That was when I realized she was a huge Peter Pan fan. Would it have killed her to name the baby Wendy?

MEET THE SIMPSONS?

Mr. Simpson had several cats named Homer, Marge, Bart, Lisa, and Wallis. Thinking myself clever, I said, "You know, the Simpson baby's name is Maggie. Wallis Simpson isn't related to the Simpsons at all."

Mr. Simpson frowned. "I'm well aware of that. For the record, Wallis Simpson is a human being, so technically not related to any fictional cartoon characters."

Red-faced, I replied, "Touché, Mr. Bond. Well played."

He stared at me blankly, without a clue to my James Bond reference. Cue the crickets. Feeling foolish, I gave up and returned to my multi-cat exam.

GERRY AND MALCOLM

One client was extremely neurotic about her cats. I had inherited Gerry and her cat Malcolm because no one else wanted to deal with her at the clinic where I worked at the time. Gerry was a hypochondriac who unfortunately latched onto me and called every day. This was back when I had patience and was inexperienced enough to let the receptionists send her calls to me. Gerry kept meticulous logs of every calorie Malcolm ate, each ounce of urine voided, and the length and width of his "waste."

I figured out a way to allow Gerry to share pertinent information only during Malcolm's visits and extricate myself from the room posthaste. Otherwise, I might have been trapped in there for hours. We also devised a system to manage Gerry if a visit went overtime. My assistant Jill would come to the door and tell me we had an emergency requiring my immediate exit and a swift end to the visit.

One day Jill was in the room with us. As we neared the end of the visit, Malcolm quite audibly passed gas. We all went silent and stared at each other, until Gerry howled in embarrassment, "I am so sorry! I don't know what to say. I think it's because he ate—"

"Everybody toots," I interrupted. This was a twist on the title of a children's book I had read many times to my children, *Everybody Poops*. While I remained stone-faced, Jill started to choke as she tried to hold back giggles and had to leave the room. We heard her laughing loudly behind the door and down the entire length of the hallway. Gerry, mortified, swiftly got up and left. It was the shortest appointment we ever had with her and Malcom.

HAROLD AND MAUDE

I had an elderly client named Clifford who was a distinguished professor emeritus at Princeton University. He was tall and soft-spoken, had a full head of silver hair, and wore either a tweed jacket or a fisherman's sweater. Clifford always brought in his two beautiful, enormous Maine coon cats, Harold and Maude. Like Clifford, both were impeccably groomed, and he clearly adored them.

One day Clifford mentioned that Maude slept in his wife's bedroom and Harold slept in his bedroom. A little more information than necessary, but fine. He asked if there was anything he could use to treat the scratches and scabbed wounds Harold inflicted on his lower legs. To better understand and address the behavior, I inquired if Harold bit or clawed him.

Clifford related that every morning, Harold clamped onto his calf and pleasured himself on Clifford's leg. I was stunned into silence. Finally, I told Clifford he should discourage the behavior. He replied that he didn't have the heart to stop Harold since the cat got so much joy out of it. I recommended thick socks, applying Neosporin to the wounds, and walked out.

SMEGMA AND OTHER PENIS EMERGENCIES

Clients often ask for an appointment when they become concerned that their dog's penis is exposed. Some are bordering on panic by the time I see them. They describe a white discharge coming from the "area" near his, "You know, his um, thingy," and ask if their pet is sick.

I assure them the discharge is completely normal, and that it has a silly name: smegma.

I wonder how many times I've clarified, "That's correct: S-M-E-G-M-A . . . No, I have no idea why it's called that . . . Yes, I agree. It is a ridiculous term, isn't it? Shall we move on now?"

I've dealt with many canine penile erectile "emergencies" where I've had to reassure pet parents that their animals are perfectly fine. But one recent call *was* a true emergency. I received multiple texts from Yolanda, a client who lived just a few doors away from me. At the time, Holden was a seven-month-old shepherd mix who weighed close to sixty-five pounds.

"Help, it's Holden," she said. "I don't know what to do. He's running around frantically in circles, licking at his penis, which is stuck out!"

A graphic photo accompanied the panicked plea.

I promised to be there momentarily and ran to the back of my house to research the condition. I recalled a lesson about it in school and knew that paraphimosis, as it is called, could be serious if the penis remained exposed. Dogs sometimes gnaw at the area in reaction to pain. In the worst cases, surgical intervention is necessary to remove exposed, damaged tissue.

I would need to return the penis to its unexposed state with lube and manual manipulation. Fabulous. Just what I wanted to do in Yolanda's backyard without an assistant to help. I loaded my backpack with a giant tube of K-Y Jelly and several latex gloves, and pedaled over on my bike.

Luckily, by the time I arrived, things had fixed themselves. I told Yolanda that sexual excitement could make the problem recur, so we needed to remove the cause of excitement. For example, if there was an intact female in the home who would repeatedly go into heat, she should be spayed. Other identified sources of arousal should also be removed.

Yolanda said the erections occurred when Holden humped his "girlfriend," a sofa pillow. She dumped the pillow in the trash, and my job there was done.

It occurred to me that if I ever had an accident and was found by paramedics or police, unconscious on the side of the road, they would wonder about the contents of my backpack: a large tube of K-Y, several gloves, and photos of a dog penis on my phone. Thankfully, the situation hasn't come to pass.

CATS: HAIRBALL AND FLEA TREATMENTS

For decades I have seen cats who vomited hairballs, and I've discussed treatments and prevention with their pet parents. In the last few years, veterinarians have collectively come to a clearer understanding of the usual cause of this upchucking—large meals. Smaller meals are better and can prevent hairball vomiting, as they more closely mimic the size of a mouse hunted in the wild.

Also, when cats self-groom, they ingest hair in the process. Clumps of hair are then brought up, along with food in the vomitus, which has trouble moving past the stomach into the smaller diameter of the intestines. This irritates the sphincter, and the material is sent backward and then out as a hairball. While the majority of cats are free-fed dry food left out in large quantities, we will continue to see hairballs.

There are diets marketed as "hairball formulas," said to prevent this problem. While some may help and others don't seem to hurt, I am not convinced that they make a big difference.

I usually recommend versions of a product called Laxatone or Petromalt. Essentially flavored Vaseline, most are formulated as a gel, come in a tube, and effectively coat the mass of hair and make it easier to pass through the intestinal tract. I dispensed it several times a week for nearly twenty years before it occurred to me that I was suggesting clients feed a petroleum product to their cats.

I had been saying, "Laxatone is a petroleum-based, flavored treatment, and comes in two flavors," and not a single client questioned it.

Think about it: I instructed people to feed their pets petroleum.

I altered my recommendations that day. Cats vomit for many reasons. Addressing and rectifying the underlying cause is the sounder medical solution, albeit not always a fast and easy one.

When I stopped recommending the quick fix, I was often met with resistance by those who were accustomed to it. Yet these same petroleum-seeking clients often refused to put chemicals on their pets in the form of topical flea preventives and preferred to feed their cats brewer's yeast and garlic to prevent fleas. While adamant about not putting perceived poisons *on* their pets, they had no problem putting poisons *into* their pets.

The converse occurs when clients prefer to feed their pets organic garlic or brewer's yeast to prevent fleas in lieu of "chemicals." In my experience, with a true flea infestation, both organic options are ineffective. Even worse, garlic is toxic to cats in higher doses, with a small margin of safety. It can cause life-threatening anemia. It is a member of the Allium family that includes onions, chives, and leeks. These are all also toxic to dogs. Clients regularly argue with me and state the alleged health benefits of the products.

Brewer's yeast is a a fungus that helps ferment beer, using grains such as barley and wheat. Its flea prevention qualities are an incidental, anecdotal finding, both for cats and dogs. I became frustrated when faced with flea-infested patients and symptoms of flea allergy dermatitis, yet the clients refused to believe flea bites were the culprit.

"It must be something else," they'd insist. "I've been giving garlic and brewer's yeast for years, and it's always helped."

One satisfying way to prove a belligerent client wrong is to point out a live flea or flea dirt, which is flea feces comprised of digested blood. When fleas bite a dog, cat, or a person, they are taking a blood meal. Flea feces resembles black specks of dirt. Placed on a white paper towel, it produces a trail of pink blood streaks when water is run over the towel.

A live flea is even more effective. This is where I am invaluable. I am a sentinel and will attract the lone flea in a room or on a pet to me. If a coworker finds themselves in this situation and hopes to point out a flea on a pet, they call me into the room.

If you have several animals in a home and a flea infestation, you may notice that only one pet carries all or most of the fleas on his or her body. After the other pets in the home are bitten, the fleas return back to the unfortunate, flea-loaded pet. You can find evidence of the dirt on all the pets, but locating the sentinel is like hitting pay dirt. Close to 100 percent of the time, I did.

One client lived with fifteen cats. All but one lived exclusively indoors. I recommended they all get flea prevention because they were at risk of exposure not only from the human beings who went in and out of the house but because of the cat who spent time outdoors. The client declined to treat all the cats. She agreed to treat the cat who went out, but only through August.

This behavior highlights another common veterinary client misconception. Summer may end in September, but flea problems don't go away, at least not in the northeastern United States, until winter. Each fall I see dogs and cats infected in late November and early December because clients stopped treatment too early. Sometime in late October and early November, the fleas hitch a ride onto their pet and relocate to the warm comfort of the home, ready to multiply in vast numbers all winter.

My recommendations to continue treatment through the end of November were not heeded by this particular client. She brought in two itchy, mostly bald cats in mid-December. I collected three jumping fleas, much to her dismay. She had ankle bites as well. I learned two other cats were at home with bald patches at the base of their tails—a classic symptom of flea bites.

The infestation was so severe she had to remove all fifteen cats, have them bathed while the home was treated, and start them all on an oral product, Capstar, for a few days to kill the live fleas.

If you have needed to purchase any of these products, I think you will agree the prevention is cheaper than the cure. And vets don't make a profit on flea preventives. I never saw this client and her cats again for flea problems.

PSYCHIC NETWORK VS. VETERINARY MEDICINE

I am open-minded to alternative therapies and go into detail about some of the ones that are effective in Chapter 14. If there is an ancillary therapy that does not interact with or contradict my medical recommendations, I am all for it. But there's a point where I draw the line.

My long-term clients Jerome and Max were beginning to frustrate me. They frequently ignored my advice, particularly for their dog HellCat. They never seemed satisfied with a successful form of treatment and were always looking for other answers or options. Case in point: they stopped giving heartworm medication and flea and tick prevention, and HellCat became infested with fleas. They were annoyed, and I was perplexed. Why change something that had worked for years?

One day I got a distressed call from Jerome. He was worried that HellCat was dying. He was convinced the dog only had weeks to live. Could I come right away?

I pressed Jerome for details. "What is HellCat doing differently? Is he lethargic? Is he eating? Did you take him to another vet who diagnosed him?"

Jerome replied, "I just know. A father knows!"

With that vague and useless history, I arrived for an examination. HellCat was his normal aggressive self, and we muzzled him without event. I saw nothing new on his exam. At a loss, I asked, "How about we do some blood work? It's been a while, and sometimes things not obvious on an exam can show up on a metabolic panel."

Jerome bellowed, "What's the point?!"

I had no idea what was wrong with HellCat until Max got home from work and enlightened me. Jerome had been consulting with a pet psychic via Zoom calls. This had been going on for years. Recently the calls were more frequent, and the predictions increasingly dire. It was the "animal intuitive," as she preferred to be called, who had suggested HellCat stop the preventatives. And the diet HellCat had loved for years was purportedly bringing in bad vibes that she could sense as far away as the West Coast.

The intuitive told Jerome that HellCat was not long for this world. Until then, Max had been unaware of how many of these consults had occurred. He became angry, and I was nearly apoplectic with frustration. I resisted the urge to rip their computer out of the wall. Instead, I gently explained that I could not do my job well if the "intuitive's" contradictory advice was being heeded over my own. They agreed to end their relationship with the intuitive, and HellCat went on to live many more years. This was not my first run-in with a kooky client. Nor was it the last.

CHAPTER 9

ECCENTRIC CLIENTS

We love our pets dearly. Yet that love can cause us to say and do the goofiest things. This chapter addresses the outliers—clients who take their love and devotion to their pets too far.

Our pets are forever babies. They never talk back, grow up, move away to college, or marry. I get perturbed if I perceive an insult directed at my dogs. I can acknowledge nutty behavior of my own, and I'm sympathetic when clients overreact if things don't go as they hope. They might be set off if asked to wait an extra day for an appointment for vaccines or several hours for a phone call with laboratory results. I would be upset too if I watched my dog or cat screech in terror or bleed while their nails are trimmed. My intent is not to shame anyone when I share actual events in this chapter. These scenarios have made for a more interesting—and on occasion, dangerous—career. I have attempted to put myself in the position of the client to see what brought them to the breaking point, in an effort to let their behavior, threats, and insults roll off my back. The stories I include about clients are so outrageous they stand out in my memory. All of them did what they did for love.

WHAT IS IT ABOUT TEETH?

The only time I had to appear in court to defend my veterinary license was after I removed a patient's diseased teeth in a dental prophylactic surgery. Prior to every dental procedure, including this case, I required all clients to sign an estimate detailing the number of teeth in need of extraction and the projected cost of the procedure. Each tooth removed means more time spent under anesthesia, a slight increased risk to the patient, and higher fees.

There is no way to be certain if a tooth needs to be removed until the patient is sedated and I've completed a thorough mouth exam and dental X-rays. Unbeknownst to me and the staff, one client expected she would have the opportunity to give us additional permission for the tooth removal mid-procedure, after the exam and X-rays.

I would never agree to this. The delay a call would cause, even if I was able to quickly reach the client, would put the patient at higher risk. Still, this woman sued me. I ultimately won the court case, brandishing the signed waiver that made her claims of malpractice null and void.

The client's reaction to the need for dental extractions wasn't unusual. Teeth are only pulled for a valid medical reason—to relieve pain, disease, and infection, which can spread to other organs, such as the heart. Countless clients have regaled me with stories of the "new, puppy-like or kitten-like" pet who emerged after their teeth were cleaned and the problematic ones removed. And yet so many others are distraught when they see their dog or cat with a gap in their mouth.

I will never comprehend why so many clients are obsessed with their pets' teeth. I've had clients request that I give them their pet's teeth after euthanasia. One couple wanted to make a necklace with the teeth. Another family wished to have four teeth removed from their dog after death so they could send one to each of their four children.

While I will never completely understand what drives people to make what I consider strange requests, I try to be professional and respectful of their wishes. But I draw the line if those wishes require me to extract teeth from a deceased pet.

SPEAKING OF UNUSUAL POSTMORTEM REQUESTS AND EVENTS

Distraught and frantic clients have been driven to some pretty disturbing reactions to their pets' deaths. One client requested I remove her cat's tail. She wanted to make it into a necklace. I declined.

Another asked me to supply them with their basset hound's ear, again for a necklace. You have me to thank for not being seated in a boat at "It's a Small World" at Disney beside a woman dangling a basset hound ear from her neck. You're welcome.

The family of a Weimaraner asked me to provide them with their deceased dog's toe, so they could "bring him everywhere with them," as a pendant.

There are services that package your deceased pet's paws, arranged in a box of dried flowers. I don't want to know how they come by the paws, as I have also declined these requests.

One client performed a necropsy (an animal autopsy) of his dog in his garage after she passed. The dog died of liver cancer, and the owner brought the liver to me in a Tupperware container in hopes I could confirm the diagnosis to give him peace of mind.

A neighbor brought her dog, who had just died, to my home for me to confirm he was truly dead. I walked out of my bedroom, freshly showered and in my robe, to see what the commotion in the foyer was. I grabbed my stethoscope and confirmed he had passed while she wailed in hysterics on the front porch. I installed security cameras the next day.

A client of mine scheduled a home euthanasia for his cat. We arrived that afternoon to find a sadly comatose patient being "kept alive" with an electric heating blanket. The client could not move forward with the procedure as planned, and rescheduled a return visit for the following day, against my wishes. I would have preferred to end the cat's suffering instead of prolonging it, but this scenario is not unusual. It puts me in a difficult position. I hate to leave, expecting another call from the client, desperate that I return immediately, typically in the middle of the night when I am simply not available. In this circumstance, I reasoned that the cat was unaware and out of pain.

I returned the next day to find that she had passed away on her own. The client shared a video he had made of her last moments, during which he administered CPR in a futile attempt to bring her back. I was appalled and surprised to find he had also posted the video on Facebook, at a time before their algorithm removed inappropriate videos such as this.

WICCA WITCHES: SALT AND TOENAILS

I did relief work at a practice where I met a colorful client named Vera and her dog, Fantasia. The dog had recurrent skin and ear infections. Vera was thrilled when my treatment resolved the issue, unlike previous vets' attempts.

I saw Fantasia on three occasions. During the second visit, Vera presented me with a large bag of salt as a gift. I thanked her and assumed it was for cooking. I later learned that Vera was a Wiccan witch, and that black salt can be used to bring forth positive energy and to protect from negativity.

Vera asked me if she could keep Fantasia's toenail shavings. Evidently nails were used in evil spells and seen as demonic.

I also learned that hair brings power and strength to those who use it in their spells. Vera told me she instantly knew I would cure her dog because of my full head of hair. She added, "You should swing your head and hair around a few times for extra good luck as a 'power boost' as the need arises."

While Vera credited the resolution of her dog's skin issues to my abundance of hair and not my training and work experience, I can't complain. I was relieved to be in her good graces, whether or not I believed in her magic. Better to have her leave on a good note.

HYPOCHONDRIACS

While I was at my position in a busy practice in New Jersey, a client brought in a Yorkie puppy for the first of several new patient visits. When the first stool sample tested positive for roundworms, it took an hour to ease my client's concerns. She was hyper-focused on the possibility of contracting worms from her dog. She could not get past scenarios of, for example, an accidental ingestion of a microscopic parasite, which could have made its way onto her jeans after the pup sat on her lap. I dreaded her visits and wondered how she would ever fully enjoy life with this pup. She canceled a follow-up visit, and I never saw her again.

A few months later, I was introduced to my daughter's friend's new puppy. The dog looked familiar. The young pup had been returned to the breeder by the previous owner under vague circumstances.

When I asked to see the dog's papers, I found my handwriting on the records. This was my former patient. The client's obsession with catching a disease caused her to return the dog, and it led the sweet puppy to a new, wonderful forever home. It was a strange coincidence but ended well.

I have a current house-call client who is neurotic about the handling and care of her two dogs. Both are severely overweight, and their health suffers as a consequence. The client is reluctant to admit the role she plays in their orthopedic issues, but I persist with my weight loss advice.

One of her dogs, Marsha, weighs thirty-two pounds, but would be healthier at eighteen pounds. Marsha has severe osteoarthritis of both knees, in part from an old, unrepaired ligament injury. Marsha's obesity exacerbates the orthopedic symptoms.

The client insists we use her own pet scale and thermometer at visits, and we must ask her permission to touch and lift the dogs at each step of the exam. I was once so exasperated, I told her, "You know, I'm a doctor."

Marsha has advanced heart and dental disease. The client declined my advice to have Marsha's teeth cleaned under anesthesia, which she fears. My attempts to explain the role the teeth play in worsening the heart were futile. I have been repeatedly frustrated with the client's refusal to acknowledge the severity of the heart condition and to have a heart specialist stabilize Marsha's heart. This, in turn, would make it safer to clean and remove any diseased teeth.

At one point, Marsha collapsed and was taken to the ER, where a cardiologist evaluated her. The specialist and I now co-manage her case, which is an enormous relief to me. The client's neuroses could have prevented me from providing proper care for Marsha.

To Neuter or Not to Neuter

Veterinarians recommend female dogs be spayed and male dogs be neutered for preventive medical reasons. Female dogs are over 90 percent less likely to develop mammary (breast) cancer if spayed before their first heat (generally just after six months of age). The cancer prevention benefit rate drops with each successive heat.

Decades ago, it was suggested a dog be spayed after her second heat cycle. Many clients continue to believe this is appropriate, and it can be a struggle to convince them otherwise, though we have long advised they have this procedure at six months of age. Dogs who've had litters can and should be spayed when older to prevent a serious health risk from a uterine infection called pyometra.

A neutered male dog won't develop testicular cancer, since he no longer has testicles. A recent large study with golden retrievers suggested the protective benefit of early neuters may not be as high as we once believed. Long-term studies have yet to demonstrate this effect in all breeds.

Neutering young male dogs can make it easier to train them, particularly if they have dominant or aggressive tendencies. Once neutered, they tend to be a bit calmer and less distracted by the presence of female dogs in heat. Many doggie day care centers ban intact dogs because hormonal influence can escalate playtime interactions.

Often breeders of large-to-giant breeds recommend and even require adoptive families to delay neutering until eighteen months to allow full physical maturation of height and muscle. Based on the golden retriever study's findings, I have no problem with neuters of dogs older than a year.

Many clients vehemently oppose spays and neuters. While there is some truth to men being more squeamish about their male dogs being "snipped," it's not only men who resist spays or neuters. Both men and women have also asked me if testicular prosthetics can be surgically placed. Aesthetics play a role for clients, clearly. Since this chapter is about outlier clients, I'll mention some of the more colorful protests.

One client, who happened to be a pediatrician, chose not to spay her Bernese mountain dog, who was critically ill with a pyometra.

"I would be taking away her choice to be a mother," she said. I might argue she was taking away her dog's choice to survive.

Another client, an elderly woman, declined my advice to spay her Chihuahua named Minnie. She claimed she loved her dog too much to do so.

"She humps her toy for twenty minutes a day," she told me. "I don't want to take this away from her."

She saw me as someone who would deprive Minnie of joy.

Several clients refused to deny their dogs the wonders and experience of motherhood. One was adamant. "I am not going to make this life decision for her!"

Another emotionally rationalized and said, "I wouldn't want someone to tell me I couldn't have kids, so I'm not going to tell her she can't."

One irate woman, deeply offended by my suggestion, yelled, "When does the dog get to choose?"

Curiously, she came in for every vaccine and treated her dog's ear infection. I presume the dog "got to choose" those treatments.

I have a German shepherd patient named Alice who has unmanaged aggression. The client has never taken my advice to pursue behavioral therapy and to spay Alice.

"I don't want to restrict or change who she is," she said.

I wondered why she had me visit at all if her plan was to continue to decline all my suggestions.

Shortly after Alice's first birthday, the client tried to nudge her off the couch. In response, Alice bit and broke the client's finger. The client asked me for a trainer recommendation the next day.

WHEN LINES OF COMMUNICATION BREAK DOWN

Most pet parents are wonderful. However, sometimes they are the problem. Some don't pay their bills. They may dispute the costs. On rare occasions, things escalate and the clients threaten me and the staff.

Such was the case with one past client, Mrs. Smith. She lived with eight pets (five dogs, three cats), all of whom were under my veterinary care. None were vaccinated regularly, nor were they given flea, tick, or heartworm preventative.

I understand that she couldn't afford all of these products for eight pets. I personally believe comprehensive care for fewer pets is better than spotty care for more pets. I supported her as best I could, though, and advised her within a framework that worked for both of us.

Sadly, in the span of three years, two of her dogs were hit by cars. When one of them was brought in after having just been struck, we performed emergency treatment and CPR as requested by the client. Unfortunately, the dog passed away, as his injuries were excessive and untreatable. The client went off the rails emotionally. She slung threats and insults at us and refused to pay her bill.

Not long after, we fired her as a client. She followed up with angry letters detailing her discontent. All of this was documented in her records.

Two years later, she called to complain because she had been turned down by a pet rescue when she attempted to adopt a dog. They had contacted us as a reference a few days prior. The ex-client suspected we told them she was an unconscientious pet owner. She wanted to speak with me directly.

"Hello, Mrs. Smith," I said as cordially as I could. "I have your record here. Please understand that the rescue only asked if you gave your dogs monthly heartworm medication, spayed or neutered them, and if they were vaccinated for rabies. You declined all of these services for the several years they were in my care. I was obliged to tell them this."

"Well, you people suck," she shot back. "We're great pet owners. We give them a good home. You should tell the rescue how many times we came in and took care of our pets when they were sick."

"Would you like me to share your records with another rescue group if they call?"

"Yes."

"You realize the records include the letter where we fired you after you threatened me and the staff. To be clear, in those records, I quoted you calling me a 'two-bit whore puppy doctor who only cares about making money.'"

"That's crazy. I didn't say that."

"That's right. It is crazy. And you did say it. And then you told the receptionist, 'You people are horrible, and I'm gonna set this clinic on fire someday,' on July 7, 2016, at 7:47 p.m. Does any of this ring a bell?"

She let out a frustrated sigh. "You had no right to fire me as a client. I quit anyway."

"That's all well and good. Would you like me to send the rescue your records along with the letter you sent us after we fired you?"

"Can you remind me what else I said in the letter?"

"Yes, it's right here. You said, 'Dr. Filos, it's ridiculous that you charged us money today when Jerry was hit by a van and then died. I don't think we should have to pay when we walked out with a dead dog. You couldn't even save him. When we ran over Matilda in our driveway a few years ago, you were able to fix her broken leg, and I was okay paying then, even though it was expensive. I am going to another practice where they won't ask me to neuter my dog and aren't full of cruel people who just want to rip me off and tell me to get vaccines. Vaccines for pets don't even work. Someday I might just come and slash your tires so you can walk home. I hope your dog gets hit by a car and you have to go to a vet and they will make you pay money to save your dog's life. It's terrible how you charge people when they have an emergency. All you care about is money.'" I waited a beat, then said, "To confirm, you want me to send the rescue group this letter."

"Yes. Make sure it shows how many times I came in."

"Will do. I'll go ahead and forward the records. Good luck with your adoption, Mrs. Smith."

A day in the life of a vet might include getting a tin of cookies and a big hug of thanks for saving the life of a beloved pet. That same day, I might also be called a money-grubbing "two-bit whore puppy doctor."

Curious to know more insider details of vet life? The next chapter is for you.

CHAPTER 10

BEHIND THE SCENES OF VET LIFE

Have you ever thought of being a veterinarian, or wondered what life is like as a vet? This book is a deep dive into the reality of such a career. It reveals all the joy, frustration, and the sometimes less-than-glamorous nature of the profession. In this chapter, I relay the day-to-day details that make my job unique and wonderful.

IN THE BEGINNING

You will need to be studious to tolerate three-plus years of day-long, back-to-back lectures in veterinary school. Settle down and get comfortable with a textbook, because early on it will be your life. Afterward and forevermore, you will be mentally and physically challenged and exhausted at the end of your workdays.

Once you graduate, you'll be greeted by one of two comments from strangers when you disclose your profession. One half will say, "I heard it was harder to get into vet school than medical school."

The other half will ask, "Do you even need to go to school for this?" They often add, "Are you a real doctor?"

This is where you will need to bite your tongue . . . or not, based on your mood. My recommended response is, "Yes, I am a real doctor, and I have the student loans to prove it."

THE NITTY AND THE GRITTY

While veterinary medicine is a wonderful career, there are some "dirty" secrets you will want to know first. By dirty, I mean just that—filth, mud, and bodily discharges. Expect to be covered in them often. If you get squeamish at the sight of brain surgery on *Grey's Anatomy*, this may not be the career for you. Personally, I hate the sight of wounds on people, but I am fine with animal injuries. If you enjoy gore, you're in for a treat. There's plenty of it, particularly if you're drawn to a career in emergency medicine or orthopedics.

While you can specialize in any discipline, such as surgery or internal medicine, most veterinarians do a bit of everything. A large portion of your cases will involve dermatological problems, often caused by allergies, but also caused by parasites. You might be surprised at how much time you spend in search of and treating external parasites, or ectoparasites (fleas, ticks, worm eggs, maggots, and mites, which cause mange). You may become hoarse after a long summer day explaining how to treat flea infestations. There are many options available to prevent external bugs, but unfortunately not every client uses them.

There is an equally vast array of internal parasites to diagnose and then expunge from pets. It would seem that vets have a fascination with feces, considering the amount of time spent discussing it and looking at it under a microscope. Several times a day, I instruct clients to collect fecal samples for their appointment and to refrigerate it until I arrive. It surprises me how many people don't know what the term "fecal sample" means. I must clarify: "a bowel movement or poopy." Others refuse to collect it and wait for me to come and procure it myself.

Parasitology proved to be the most boring, yet ultimately most relevant, class in vet school. James Herriot could have easily written another version of his best-selling book and retitled it *All Critters Big and Small.*

MORE ON THE YUCK FACTOR

My profession is rife with not just dirt, blood, and gore but also smells and sights that assault the senses. Many of us vets enjoy what most would consider vile. I do not shy away from videos and photos shared by veterinarians on social media: *Cuterebra* larvae (big, ugly worms) as they poke out of a wound; giant ruptured sebaceous adenomas (enormous pimples); large, long sticks being pulled out of a cat's eye, leg, or other body part.

I get a thrill when I find ear mites under a microscope and magnify them onto a screen to share with the client. The grosser they are, the greater the satisfaction. Clients seem less interested in knowing the details, so I'm forced to share my findings with colleagues. I am repulsed by maggots and am not a fan of giant anal gland abscesses, but for the most part, I was born for this.

If you've watched *Dirty Jobs* with host Mike Rowe, you might agree there aren't many dirtier jobs than being a vet. We stick our hands in orifices all day long. Bodily fluids tend to get everywhere. I have had saliva, blood, pus, and earwax flung into my eyes and mouth.

Vets are constantly forced to inspect vomitus. We interrogate clients not just about what it looked like, but how active the vomiting was, how many times the animal vomited, whether or not there was blood in it, and if the pet brought up any pills, toys, socks, etc.

For all these reasons, I bathe at least once a day. My family has put up with this for decades, and I have worked out a system to wash away any olfactory evidence of details of my workday.

THE SOCIAL NETWORK

While there are far more pros than cons associated with being a vet, some aspects of working with the public are simply trying and frustrating. For example, many people refer to the Internet to self-diagnose their pets' ailments before coming to me. I refer to them as "Dr. Google" clients. Many see their "research" as evidence that they know as much, if not more than, I do. They only realize they are wrong when it is too late. (I cherish a mug I was given that bears the warning: "Do not confuse your Google search with my medical degree.")

Some other not-so-encouraging truths about my much-loved profession:

- You will be paid less than physicians.
- Social media and online reviews can and will attack your business and you personally. You cannot please everyone, especially those who have had an unfortunate outcome and blame you or someone who works for you.
- Depression and suicide rates are higher among vets than in the general population (Brscic 2021).

I have been known to go to social events and lie about my line of work. I read the room and sense if it's the type of crowd that could pin me into a corner and line up for free pet advice. It helps to make up a fake job, such as an auditor for the IRS. Nobody wants to think about being audited. The conversation shifts direction rapidly. I say this from experience.

ENDLESS VARIETY

I wouldn't share stories from my thirty years of practice if I didn't love my work. There are many perks—there is endless variety, mental stimulation, and the satisfaction of making a difference in the lives of my patients and their families. The majority of clients appreciate my efforts, and most workdays I reflect on how fortunate I am to do what I do.

For instance, guest lecturing for each of my children's classes was always fun. And I cherished the chance to follow patients from puppy and kittenhood to old age while I lived in their neighborhoods and met them on the street or at the park.

I'm happy to give advice whenever I'm able. I've been called to assist with all things pet and wildlife. If someone wants to know what to do with an abandoned deer in their yard, they phone me. I figured out how to treat my neighbor's ducks after a fox attacked them. I've helped coax cats from trees.

I've been honored to help out friends or acquaintances at one of the most desperate times of their lives. I have received countless early morning, tear-filled voicemails when someone's pet is experiencing an end-of-life emergency. While an unexpected way to start the day, I am happy to help and make a small difference in their crises.

Of course, animal emergencies do not limit themselves to bankers' hours. After-hours calls can be exhausting and irksome. If they need you, they will call . . . text . . . come over. Plan on unexpected pop-ins and text messages to arrive after you're in your pajamas, cuddled up with your family to watch a movie, or out for dinner with friends. For this reason, never give your address or personal phone number to clients. Most clients are respectful, and usually it is not a problem. However, it can quickly turn into an invasion of privacy.

If you do become a veterinarian, be very careful about what you disclose on social media. You will get many friend requests on Facebook, followed by immediate instant messages or posts seeking veterinary advice. They will want second opinions, usually for free. Family will also offer your services to anyone and everyone they know. "Call my sister, aunt, cousin . . . Dawn. She's our vet."

Some off-hour calls are more urgent than others. Late one Sunday afternoon, I got a call from my friend Kerry. She was mildly concerned about her daughter Laura, who, several hours earlier, had been bitten on the foot by a raccoon. I was much more alarmed by her news.

Kerry asked, "Is it a big deal? The only reason I called is because her toe, which was bruised at first, is now swollen and purple."

Close to speechless, I calmly instructed her, "Drop what you're doing right now and head to the ER. Run, don't walk."

Laura has me to thank for the rabies injections she endured. And possibly also for her life!

JAMES AND THE GIANT TURTLE

One afternoon my nine-year-old neighbor James came to the door. He needed my help with a turtle. I envisioned a small box turtle who had lost his way. But as I turned the corner, I found a group of children and two adults standing around an enormous snapping turtle in the middle of the street. He must have weighed fifty pounds and was close to three feet around.

The closer I got, the worse he smelled, and the angrier he became. I told everyone to step away from him. I assumed he had a broken leg and probably an infection, both valid reasons for the rank odor and his inability to move. It would be dusk soon, and I worried a car would run him over, leaving behind a gruesome scene.

I grabbed a large snow shovel from my garage, intending to lift or sweep the turtle off the road and into the nearby creek. As soon as I poked him, he stood and charged at me. I lunged and "fenced" at him, guiding him away and back to the adjacent water basin he'd come from.

My husband, Dave, drove slowly by on his way home from work. As I waved the yellow shovel above my head and did my version of Rocky Balboa's happy dance, the assembled crowd jumped up and down and cheered for me.

Dave's face read, *What on earth have you done now?*

It made for some fun dinner conversation, and I was temporarily the neighborhood hero.

WHEN FAMILY AND WORK CONVERGE

My young son Chris and I went to an organic farm where we were members. Everyone was familiar with the resident dog, a pointer named Jack, who we found collapsed on his side in the middle of the road, blocking traffic in both directions.

As Chris watched, I assessed Jack. A small crowd formed around me as I checked his gums and listened to his heart with my stethoscope. I found no broken bones or obvious physical problems.

Several concerned bystanders asked, "What's wrong with Jack, Doc?"

I had no clue. I gave him a little pat on the rump, and he popped up and trotted away as the group erupted in applause.

Chris clapped and beamed at me. "Mommy, you saved him!"

I drove away as fast as I could. Only I knew I had just rescued poor Jack from a mid-summer day's nap.

STAR FOR A DAY

I have poor hand-eye coordination and was always the last person to be selected for sports teams. But I do have remarkably quick reflexes, and sometimes a little bit of luck. One day my family was at the soccer fields where six-year-old Chris was playing a game. In youth soccer, the size of the fields get bigger as the children age. There were at least twelve simultaneous games spread out over the expanse of grass, which covered the distance of two football fields. Spectators stood or sat in chairs, subdividing the games like human fences.

We were located at one end, next to the main road. People from the far end of the other side started running toward us. It took me a moment to realize they were chasing a dog, trailing his leash and sprinting with abandon, as if he had just robbed a bank. As he passed through each team's area of play, everyone stopped and watched him. The reaction resembled a small "wave" you might see in the stands at a stadium.

This dog adeptly avoided capture and passed through game after game. We watched as he—was it my imagination?—beelined directly toward me. I sat in my lawn chair mesmerized as—was this also in my mind?—he and I locked eyes. The distance between us closed. I was the end of the line for this pup, and several hundred people knew it.

He ran directly to my left side. In the smoothest, coolest gesture I have ever made, I leaned over and deftly scooped up the end of his leash. Ear-splitting applause and cheers followed as I calmly stood and handed him to his out-of-breath and thankful family. I believe the dog wanted to be caught. To my family, I was a star for the day.

HONEY, HOW WAS YOUR DAY?

My family knows better than to ask about the details of my day at the dinner table, as so many stories are either gross or hard to explain. Sometimes, as in the story above, I impress my children. Other times I appall them.

One day I shared a story about my long-term client named Mike and his pit bull terrier, Puma. I adored Puma, who was seventy-eight pounds of pure love and drool. He was rescued from a career as a fighter and had multiple scars, both physical and emotional. His appearance could be daunting, but it masked the cream puff I knew lived in the body of this scary-looking dog.

Mike once brought Puma in to see me after returning from a weekend visit with family. Puma drooled and pawed at his mouth in obvious pain. Mike believed there was a bone lodged in Puma's mouth. Mike is an emotional person who has never allowed Puma to be sedated. He'd had another dog pass away while in surgery, and he never allowed another of his pets to undergo surgery, nor to be neutered.

I understood Mike's long-standing fears, but the poor ER doctor he saw while out of town did not. Apparently, Mike yelled accusations, including speculations about the doctor's manhood. Mike histrionically relayed the scene to me. He'd refused anesthesia, which would have enabled the vet to examine Puma's mouth more thoroughly.

He told the ER vet, "When I get home, I'm taking Puma to his regular vet, a woman half your size. She's close to five feet tall, and is ten times braver than you'll ever be!"

For the record, I'm 5 feet 2¾ inches tall.

We huddled on the floor, without the aid of anesthesia. Mike pried Puma's considerable jaws open. Wedged between the dog's upper teeth, against his hard palate, was a soup bone, roughly an inch wide and four inches long. I had to move my head into Puma's mouth to adequately see the bone. I yanked it out as gently and quickly as I could. Puma immediately rolled over and bestowed grateful wet kisses upon me. I was touched by his visible display of thanks.

Only later that evening, when I relayed the story to my slack-mouthed, appalled husband, did I stop to think about what could have gone wrong during the appointment. While I trusted both Mike and Puma, my decision to skip anesthesia was made in haste.

Stranger Danger

Another story not appropriate for dinner conversation revolved around a stranger's dog. Many times, I've stopped my car on the road to help a roaming dog or even wildlife that seems in imminent harm. Yet not everyone is grateful for my unsolicited assistance. That day, while driving on a busy road in the pouring rain, I saw a trembling Yorkie, soaked and wandering near the road at the end of a long, steep driveway. I pulled over in my van, scooped him up, and drove to the house.

I was greeted by his owner and another dog, a wet and muddy chocolate Labrador retriever. I opened the doors of my van, which had a beige interior, to allow the man to retrieve his Yorkie.

My good deed did not go unpunished. Not only was the man displeased with the Yorkie, he didn't bother to thank me. And his Labrador jumped in and bounced around the van, covering both rows of seats in mud.

When I shut the doors and left, I smelled a strong odor. The brown mess wasn't just mud. It was something far worse and "organic." I detailed the car for hours afterward.

Now I'll Take Questions, Comments, and Strange Requests

I get many questions and requests from clients or acquaintances, often oddball and entertaining. It's rare when I have to decline to help, but when I do, there is a very good reason.

One client asked, "While Nemo is here to be neutered, may we take pictures of him while he's asleep before you take him to surgery? We want to dress him up in a Santa suit for our holiday card photo."

"Oh, sure," I replied sarcastically. "Why don't you bring the entire family and a photographer too? I'll simply give him more sedative until you get the perfect shot."

"Are you serious? Could we do that?" the unwitting client said. "Wouldn't that be dangerous?"

I shook my head vehemently. "No, I'm not serious! And yes, it would be dangerous and ridiculous."

"So that's a no, then?" the client asked. "No pictures?"

WHAT GOES DOWN, SOMETIMES COMES UP

One of my clients wondered why her dog was vomiting. Her comments made me smirk.

"I haven't given him anything out of the ordinary to eat," she said. "Unless you count the fried eggs and bacon I fed him yesterday. Could that make him sick?"

I sighed. "Yes, bacon can definitely make him sick. It's high in fat and can cause gastroenteritis or even pancreatitis. Please, no more bacon. Period."

"But it's organic," she protested.

I shook my head. "Organic fat is fat, and it's still a problem."

Conversations like this reinforce my love for the job—medicine with a side of entertainment.

DOC, DID YOU GET MY TEXTS?

As I mentioned, I sometimes get texts that pertain to found animals or wildlife. A dog has been found by the side of the road, or a deer, baby rabbit, opossum, snake, or dead raccoon is on the lawn. It is my pleasure to assist, with a few exceptions.

One such request came on Mother's Day when an acquaintance asked me to come and "put down" several five-week-old chicks. She had accidentally purchased "meat chicks" in lieu of the cute pet chicks she had in the past. Evidently, they grew more swiftly than expected, and their bodies outweighed what their tiny legs could support. It was inhumane to watch them, and she chickened out (her words) in her attempts to kill them herself, so she texted me. I referred her to a beef and dairy farm nearby and salvaged the remains of my holiday.

AT YOUR SERVICE

I provide a concierge-type service for my longtime clients. Cell phones, and the ability to text, lighten the load of my daily practice. Texting offers an efficient way of giving negative test results—a single text exchange can save us from playing countless hours of phone tag. One disadvantage, however, is that people are less inhibited about sending a text than making a call. This has ruined many a holiday family dinner, where I have frequently received photos of tick bites, vomitus, diarrhea, wounds, or even a prolapsed rectum. But the advantages far outweigh the downside.

Some unintended miscommunications are a direct result of texting. Many of them have come from my end when I inadvertently send out the wrong message, or an unedited text, to a client. The converse is also true. I also occasionally receive texts intended for someone else. I've been sent shopping lists. A client once told me he loved me, only to realize he meant to give that message to his wife. After clarification, we all had a good laugh.

Voice transcriptions, combined with autocorrect, often lead to garbled messages and result in some embarrassing situations. I have lived to regret the terrible habit I have of neglecting to proofread messages and had to deal with the consequences later. These scenarios motivated me to write an essay, while enraged at technology. I've included a section of it here.

Dear Autocorrect,

I am a veterinarian, not a "vegetarian" or a "vegan again." Why, oh why, do you make these inane substitutions? And for the record, when I refer clients to my blog, it is to Dr. Dawn the Pet Vet, not "pervert." Is this an intentional attempt to embarrass me? Similarly, did you earn extra credit for your correction of my business name from Bucks Mercer Mobile Vet to "big fat mobile vet"?

Please enlighten me as to why you swap entire sentences and sentiments. I once texted to notify a client I was running a bit late for their appointment, and instead sent, "I am coming to get laid for your appointment." Hilarious.

I am sure you got a real kick out of when I texted, "We are sitting in your driveway," and it was sent as "We are shi**ing in your driveway."

Thank you. From the bottom of my fart . . . I mean heart!

✦ ✦ ✦

One group of people I can never ignore is family. Their requests come fast and furious at all hours of the day and night, and especially on holidays. They may be the most eccentric of all. You be the judge in the next chapter.

CHAPTER II

YOU'VE GOT TO LOVE FAMILY

I take pet ownership, or pet parenting, very seriously. It's not only my profession but also my passion. Many people fail to realize the lasting effects, sacrifices, and costs of adoptions when they impulsively bring home a dog or cat. When it comes to my family, I'm extra cautious because my children are always eager to adopt a puppy, usually a trendy breed that requires frequent veterinary visits. The problem is, since I'm the only veterinarian in the family, their pet problems become *my* problems. My twenty-something daughters often call me wishing to adopt what I refer to as the breed of the week . . . a Pomsky, New Yorkie, or Frenchie are good examples. Yet I know that the brunt of the responsibility for those canine genetic superstorms will fall on me.

I regularly field texts such as, *How do you feel about Dalmatians? Are they good for small Brooklyn apartment living? How about Irish setters? What are your thoughts on bulldogs? Do Labradoodles need to be groomed?*

And, *But Mom, everyone in Brooklyn has at least one dog. I need one!*

My response: *What you need is to move out of Brooklyn!*

While my comments may seem harsh, let me share just the

tip of the extended family veterinary iceberg of assistance I have given in the last few years, in addition to my day job.

My parents' two dogs yelp and screech so loudly that I can't have a conversation with them without holding the phone far from my ears. They misinterpret my abundant advice to leave the dogs by themselves, in their respective crates, allowing the dogs to learn independence, and to prevent "COVID puppy" syndrome: a common occurrence in puppies adopted during the pandemic. Due to social isolation, these pets have been exclusively with their owners and have become emotionally dependent on the constant presence of their pet parents. They show separation anxiety with howling, barking, and often destructive behavior when they feel abandoned in the home.

My parents have created their own extreme version of the syndrome. Only one of my parents can leave the house at a time. They haven't been out to a restaurant in over two years. The dogs bark at cats, the moon, swaying palm trees, and mail carriers. My training advice was ignored. They have been reluctant to travel and leave the dogs behind with a sitter, yet are equally afraid to fly with the dogs, who will no doubt bark at flight attendants, beverage carts, and other people while on an airplane. At this rate, my parents will never be able to visit and see my new home.

My cousin has a similar problem. Her dog manifests his anxiety when she tries to leave the home with one of the worst examples of destructive separation anxiety I have encountered in thirty years. She's had to replace wall-to-wall carpeting, which was repeatedly soiled due to her dog's stress colitis. Her kitchen wall needs new Sheetrock because her dog scratched through the wall when left at home by himself for several hours. My cousin has been resistant to training with antianxiety medication, and essentially has lived under house arrest. She took a job working from home because she had no other choice. We spoke twice a week, until I changed my phone number.

My brother's dog was impaled by an arrow while hunting in Alaska. His veterinarian and I spoke twice a day for over a week.

Another cousin moved to England with her golden retriever. The steps and instructions issued by the USDA's Animal and Plant Health Inspection Service—including specifically timed microchip ID placement, rabies vaccinations, and an approval process that required obtaining an official seal—were time-consuming and frustrating. Don't get me started on the preflight tapeworm treatments. It got so bad I could barely bring myself to watch the final season of *The Crown*. The process is one I hope to never be involved in again, professionally or personally.

While my family keeps me busy, they are also supportive and a constant source of inspiration. They provide me with a steady supply of challenging problems to solve and colorful stories to share. As a group, we sometimes go to extremes—myself included. My story would be incomplete if I didn't share the eccentric misadventures of our pets . . . beginning with my own.

COACH

Coach was a chocolate Labrador retriever, adopted from a nearby breeder while I was in my second year of vet school. While I adored him, he was one of the dumbest dogs I've encountered. He did the craziest things, including eating soap bars and rolled newspapers. He once devoured an entire loaf of freshly baked bread while my head was turned to unload the dishwasher.

Once I took him to a local vet's office to have his abdomen x-rayed, hoping to find a lost set of keys. The receptionist was taken aback by my request when I phoned, but once I told her he was a Labrador, she fit us in within the hour. I cannot take credit for giving the nickname "Hoover" to Labrador retrievers, but it's spot-on. They're like vacuums in their dietary indiscretion and eating habits.

I once treated a Labrador patient for bloat after he ate fifteen pounds of dry dog food. We induced him to vomit, and the entire fifteen pounds came right back up. This is something I would not put past Coach and his passion for food. All of his kibble was kept high up on a shelf, in a latched thick plastic container.

Labrador retrievers are commonly selected to serve as guide and support dogs. Their wonderful temperament and willingness to please allows them to be easily trained. While Coach lacked intelligence, he was devoted to pleasing me. It also made him an A+ pupil in his behavior class. Coach gladly sat for several minutes until told to come. He would heel, lie down, and give me a high five any day of the week. He generously allowed my children to dress him in outfits and endured them as they painted his nails with pink polish.

My six-year-old nieces walked him through a horse show for several hours, and he neither pulled nor barked at the numerous horses, other dogs, and hordes of people he encountered. While this might have overstimulated most other dogs, Coach had already assumed the role of protector of all children from living with my daughters. True to his nature, he valiantly guarded them through the throngs. He was a big, clumsy oaf. Despite his size and knack for constantly knocking over my toddlers with his long tail, both girls learned to walk.

My daughter Gabriella always gave him a kiss goodbye as she said, "Bye-bye, Toach. I wuv you."

He certainly "wuvved" her, as he did all of us.

At the practice where I worked, I was known as Coach's mom. He boarded there often when we went out of town. Sadly, while on a trip to visit family, I was notified that Coach unexpectedly passed away overnight. He was twelve years old. My husband and I were devastated. Because I was in such shock, I did not ask for a necropsy to determine the exact cause of death. Since I knew Coach had died in his sleep, I chose to assume it was peaceful and painless.

We struggled for weeks with how to tell our three- and five-year-old daughters. They cried briefly and did not seem to process the news. Moments later, they asked if we could get a bird. Of course, they missed Coach terribly once they realized he wasn't coming back.

GEORGIA

Soon after we lost Coach, we moved, so we waited until we were settled into our new home to adopt our next dog, Georgia. She was a "mellow yellow" Labrador. She was much easier to raise and train, even while my young children habitually let her into the basement before they took her out to relieve herself in the yard.

I like an aphorism about Labradors and their infamous shedding. They only shed two times a year—six months in the summer and six months in the winter. It's funny, but accurate.

I give this advice to clients with Labrador puppies: Change your furniture to a color that matches your dog. You will not get ahead of it unless you make a commitment to vacuum every day. I purchased a beige interior minivan and cream-colored couches to match Georgia's hair. She wasn't allowed on the furniture, but it didn't matter. Her hair was everywhere. Labrador lovers will understand. I knew better than to have a dark couch and a yellow dog.

Georgia's life was shortened by serious health issues. It is a cruel and not uncommon fate of pets of veterinarians—medical misfortune seems more common in my pets and those of many of my colleagues than in the general population. I call it "Vet Pet Syndrome." Georgia became close to 100 percent blind at six years old from a disease called progressive retinal atrophy (PRA).

We had adopted Georgia before a genetic test became available to detect this eye disease. Breeders now use it to selectively remove the genetic trait from their line of dogs. While all purebreds are prone to certain genetic hereditary diseases, only some diseases have tests to predict carriers. Scrupulous breeders attempt to breed out diseases such as hip dysplasia.

It's important to do the research necessary to determine if your puppy's parents are certified clear of the diseases the breed is more prone to have. While the odds of mixed breeds carrying a genetic disease are lower, due to dilution of the chance of expression of a disease, it is impossible to know with 100 percent accuracy that they won't get the disease.

Georgia's blindness was not painful, nor was she emotionally changed by her blindness. Initially, we were distraught. Several groups and websites offer advice and support for families with blind dogs. We made a number of helpful changes to Georgia's lifestyle with the help of the Facebook pages Blind Dog Support, Blind Dog Rescue Alliance, and www.blinddogs.com.

Suggestions include adopting another pet if you don't have one already and placing a jingling bell or tag on the other dog. The blind pet will follow the other pet around the house and the yard. They also suggest that the people in the house wear bells—with a different sound, to avoid confusion—so they can be located more easily as well. Don't rearrange furniture, as sight-impaired pets memorize home layouts. Clients often realize the extent of visual impairment in their pets only after they move furniture around and the pets bump into it.

Unfamiliar environments can cause the pet distress. Elderly pets with cloudy eyes caused by an age-related condition known as nuclear sclerosis (similar to cataracts) may show these symptoms as well. The sites encourage clicker training to give audible cues to prompt your dog to sit, stay, etc.

Georgia had mainly been trained with hand gestures and needed to be retrained with voice commands. We added rugs to help her with her footing and alert her to the location of her water and food bowls.

We also got her a "halo." Products such as the Halo Vest, Walkin' Halo Harness, Muffin's Halo, and Walkin' Blind Dog Halo are marketed as a bumper between the dog and obstacles. Also known as a "white cane for blind dogs," they resemble a small Hula-Hoop that surrounds the dog's head. Who knew the world needed four types of blind dog halo contraptions? Or do we? Another example of the vast options of pet care tools available.

Just before we got Georgia a halo, she began to have severe seizures. None of the medications I tried helped, and she worsened with time. Georgia panicked and barked for an hour or more after most seizures. I attached a leash to her and sat with her while she circled and paced, disoriented. It distressed our entire family.

Further testing confirmed the worst: the episodes were caused by a brain tumor. We said goodbye to her shortly before her seventh birthday.

INDIA

Our bad luck with Labradors and purebreds led us to adopt a smaller, mixed-breed dog. Enter India, the wonder dog. India is Cavanese—half Cavalier King Charles spaniel and half Havanese. She inherited the sweet personality of Cavaliers but unfortunately also heart disease (mitral valve prolapse) common to the breed. She's doing extremely well on her medications. She loves to hunt, roll in, and then eat dead animals, an instinct inherited from both breeds.

India is a good representative of the Havanese "Velcro" description: she sticks closely to our sides and is sturdy, friendly, and affectionate. She requires regular haircuts and grooming. As I already mentioned, I am horrible at it and leave it to the professionals. While India loves to roll in dirt and malodorous detritus, she doesn't shed and is allowed on all furniture with one exception: her frequent excursions through poison ivy and mud ended any chance of her sleeping in our beds.

My daughter Isabella forever asks to host India in New York City, a few hours away. Her visits cause quite a social stir, and India is frequently invited to dog picnics and get- togethers.

Isabella is representative of many millennials and is the picture of a newly minted "adulting" child, a few years out of college. Her demographic grew up in the computer age, with the concurrent shift to the anthropomorphizing of pets. For many, their pets have largely replaced children in the years now devoted to career, travel, and experiencing life before the commitment to marriage and parenthood. Instagram, Facebook, and TikTok accounts are devoted to their pets.

COVID-19 forced Isabella to spend several months at home with us. She devoted much time to caring for India. After long hikes, she diligently removed ticks from India with hypochondriacal fervor.

I often overheard her comments.

"See how you have no ticks when I walk you? Mommy isn't as careful as I am."

Lovely. Thank you for the endorsement.

One night I was preparing dinner without my reading glasses on while simultaneously fending off Isabella's rapid-fire updates on the tick count. After her unsuccessful attempts to remove one persistent tick, I caved in, put down my spatula, and grabbed my tweezers.

Cue the soundtrack of *Jaws* as the shark approaches the boat . . . There I stood, poised to pluck off a nipple. I am happy to say I reached for my glasses, realized my error, and stopped myself just in time. It became a teaching moment. I pointed out to Isabella that India had seven more nipples just like it. I gave my patented talk: "All mammals have nipples, even men." Crisis averted.

Isabella fact-checked on Google, as my thirty years of veterinary experience wasn't sufficient proof. It brought to mind a similar incident years before when I stopped her frantic efforts to pluck off a mole on her belly that she also believed was a tick. Luckily, I was there to avert two bloody, minor disasters.

MIXED BREEDS

India has a great life, but she isn't necessarily pampered. Her medical needs are vast and more than adequately attended to, but she is not a well-dressed, clean, sweet-scented, decked-out-in-bows-and-pearls sort of dog. She is a giant, muddy hunting dog trapped in the body of a twenty-two-pound cute white Cavanese mutt. Today, to be politically correct, I should say "mixed breed."

This is a subject where I feel the need to dive deeper. No one seems to use the term "mutt" anymore. I made no comment when I met my new patient, a pugglechon (a pug, beagle, and bichon frise mix . . . spun into a "designer breed"). I prefer to use the term "mixed breed," or beagle mix, pug mix, etc.

I am amused by the names given to some dogs. Bassador (basset hound and Labrador retriever), Alusky (Alaskan malamute and Siberian husky), and bull-pei (bulldog and shar-pei) stand out.

The term "breeding" can be stretched to mean very different things. The complicated nature of genetics can produce varied presentations and sizes of a newly established combo-breed, so we add adjectives in a further attempt to legitimize the new breed: think micro, mini, teacup, micro-mini, and giant Labradoodles, when there used to be only three (mini, medium, and standard).

Because there are several sizes of poodles (standard, miniature, and toy), the size of the mixes also vary, as can the colors. Australian Labradoodles alone come in fourteen different colors! Terms such as F1, or first filial generation (the offspring of two contrasting genotypes, aka a Labrador retriever bred to a poodle), and F2, the result of a subsequent breeding of Labradoodle to Labradoodle, are used not just by dog breeders but also by the general public.

It can get complicated. A recent new puppy visit: Carly, was a chocolate Australian Labradoodle F4, a fourth filial generation of Labradoodle inbreeding. Also, consider another puppy I saw named Felicia: F1B caramel Labradoodle. Here the *B* stands for backcrossing, meaning a Labradoodle was bred with a poodle to improve coat type and increase the odds of getting a curlier, and thus more desirable, coat in the puppies.

In terms of genetics, there are times when I am less educated than the clients. For this reason, I take great care in how I phrase things, such as the breed. And pet parents are easily perturbed if their adored pet is referred to as untrained, poorly trained, or undertrained.

DID YOU CALL MY DOG FAT?

Another major faux pas is to use the word "fat." I won't say, "Your dog is fat." I am more inclined to say, "Let's reevaluate Bingo after he has lost fifteen pounds and see if he needs to drop a bit more."

Any suggestion of a client's culpability in the pet's weight problem is best avoided. Instead, I cautiously mention that their beautiful (or is it handsome?) kitty Cheerio is headed toward obesity with a weight gain of three pounds per year. To remain on this trajectory is to walk a path straight to diabetes. Simply uttering the word "diabetes" often creates a stunned silence. As it sinks in, I follow up with, "It's not a question of if but when Cheerio will become a diabetic."

But I get it. I, too, am guilty of oversensitivity to critical comments aimed at my dog. It's fine if *I* say my dog is fat, but no one else is entitled to say it to me.

An exterminator once treated our home and casually commented, "What a cute little chubster your puppy is."

Pardon? Did you just call my dog FAT? I was infuriated. I felt like he was judging not only my dog but also my pet parenting.

VETS ARE PET PARENTS TOO

The term "pet parent" emerged in the last decade and is now in the mainstream vernacular. It changes the dynamic of the relationship, replacing the term "pet owner." In the eyes of the law, pets are still considered the property of the "owner," but this view is slowly evolving with time, as pet custody cases become more common. Emotionally, society reacts more and more as parents would when faced with separation from their actual children.

My irrational response to an offhanded comment directed at my dog and, by extension, me, reflects my assumed role as India's "parent." It happens all the time. When a family member asked why India didn't accompany me everywhere for errands, I interpreted this as a direct criticism of me. Am I a bad pet parent because I don't sleep in bed with my dog? Am I seen as a poor example if my dog's nails are too long or she has bad breath? I could brush her teeth more and groom her better, but does my lack of perfectionism make me a negligent pet parent? I don't think it does, nor do I think it of my clients.

I suspect people hold me to a higher standard because of my profession, so that's part of what's happening here, though I see this type of judgment more often in society in general too. For this reason, I select words carefully as I relay medical and dietary advice to clients. If you relate to these feelings, I get you. Honestly, I do.

I understand how my dog's health care reflects on my medical capabilities. If there were a test for just that, I would pass with flying colors. But with regard to behavioral recommendations, I admit negligence and readily joke about how poorly my dog India is trained. The word "spoiled" comes up repeatedly. India will sit and roll over onto her side. Period.

A dog sitter asked India to give her her paw yesterday. I squirmed in embarrassment as India stared quizzically at her, and then me, as if to ask, "Paw? Am I supposed to know this word?" I blame it on a combination of her stubbornness and our laziness. But here again, only I am allowed to call her untrained.

Yes, India claims every couch, pillow, and lap in the home. She demands treats and silently begs for them with her eyes. She has us fully trained. But because she gives us such joy, I am okay with her being spoiled.

I completely understand if you spoil your pet as well. Our pets serve as an emotional anchor in our unpredictable lives. They are a cure for loneliness, and never more so than in the lives of senior clients, who often live alone with their pets.

CHAPTER 12

SENIOR PET PARENTS

My love of working with senior pet parents began during my last year of veterinary school. We rotated through different clinical disciplines in the teaching hospital, progressively becoming more comfortable with medicine, surgery, and most important, client communication, an art that can take a long time to master. We fourth-year students acted as intermediaries between the doctor managing the case and the client. It was our responsibility to relay updates on medical situations in terminology our clients could understand. It was also our job to interpret and pass along the clients' thoughts, concerns, and additional questions to the doctors.

That year I was introduced to several elderly clients, many of whom were widows or widowers. They shared with me their deep emotional connections to their pets. I struggled to limit those conversations to a reasonable amount of time, as I had many other duties too. But the senior pet parents I worked with deeply affected me. I had the sense I had made a difference in their lives that extended far beyond the medical care of their dog or cat.

One client, a widow named Florence, shared that her miniature schnauzer, Eleanor, was the sole link to her deceased husband. Eleanor was admitted to the veterinary hospital critically ill with respiratory disease secondary to terminal cancer. Florence understood that Eleanor didn't have much time but encouraged us to do all we could to keep Eleanor alive as long as possible. This involved extensive care, including placing Eleanor on a respirator for several days in the ICU, followed by three weeks in the medical unit. I knew losing Eleanor would have an enormous adverse psychological impact on Florence. It reinforced for me that veterinarians don't only help the patient but the family as well.

Each evening during Eleanor's first hospitalization, I bent the visiting hours rules and arranged for Florence to visit with Eleanor. I took extra time to chat with Florence, answer her questions, and for "hand-holding," a term for the extra TLC some people need.

Eleanor made it through her first hospital stay but returned several months later with end-stage disease. We humanely euthanized her two days later. This was an agonizing decision for Florence, but ultimately in Eleanor's best interest. I listened to a few more of Florence's stories before we said goodbye.

Florence has inspired me throughout my career to make sure I take the time to explain and listen to my clients' concerns. While my staff doesn't always appreciate it, my extra-long phone calls with clients are important to them and to me. People need to be given time and adequate information to understand their pets' medical conditions so they can make the best care decisions.

PSYCHOLOGICAL AND PHYSIOLOGICAL BENEFITS OF PETS

The COVID-19 lockdown demonstrated how crucial pets are to physically and psychologically enhancing our daily lives. The physical reward of getting more exercise as you walk a dog is just the tip of the iceberg. Studies published in psychology journals have shown that the act of stroking or petting a pet decreases blood pressure and heart rate (Teo 2022). It can help regulate breathing and decrease muscle tension. Pet owners have lower triglyceride and cholesterol levels than they did before they adopted pets. Playing with a pet has been shown to increase oxytocin, also referred to as a "happiness hormone." And it can lower cortisol levels, another indicator of reduced stress, as pets help relax and calm us (Cherniack 2014; Teo 2022).

Other research shows that being an animal caretaker protects against anxiety (Bolstad 2021). The elderly who live alongside pets are less lonely and depressed. Dementia and Alzheimer's patients' stress levels are lower and outbursts are fewer when they live with pets (Opdebeeck 2021). These are just some of the ways a home shared with pets can enrich our lives. It is no wonder we form such deep connections with them and see them as an extension of ourselves (Grajfoner 2021).

That connection is one of the reasons a veterinary career appealed to me. When I worked in clinics, I made sure I took the time to listen to my clients' concerns and thoroughly explain their pets' medical conditions. To drive home the issues discussed in the exam, I wrote documents reiterating my points, so clients could read them later at home. In the hopes of having more efficient conversations the next time we spoke, I tried to anticipate questions they might ask in these notes. Common questions I addressed included whether a drug would cause their pet to stop eating, exactly how deep to go when cleaning out infected ears, and whether or not it's normal for a pet's incision to look a certain way while healing.

Often when owners feel unsure of themselves and are reluctant to call the doctor to have directions repeated or explained, they err on the side of caution and skip administering treatments or giving medications. This can delay a cure or, in rare circumstances, result in more serious illness or even death.

The more complicated the situation, the higher the likelihood a pet parent will not hear or understand everything said by the doctor in the office. I repeat instructions and ask if a client understands before the appointment is over. Senior clients, especially, can become overwhelmed with detailed dosing schedules, for example. They do well with charts prepared so they can cross off treatments, or with daily pill dispensers. These clients and their needs are a large reason I started a mobile practice.

I was surprised at how many of my elderly clients live on their own in single family homes. Most do not drive. The majority have disabilities or illnesses ranging from chronically debilitating to terminal. Some are blind, and others live in nursing homes while suffering from physical maladies and memory issues. All of them are completely devoted to their pets. In most circumstances, their dogs or cats are their lifelines.

They all have described their pets with the same sentiment: "I don't know what I would do without him/her." Each time I hear this, my heart breaks a little. I don't know how they would get along without their pets either.

It's never easy to say goodbye to a pet, but young children's lack of life experiences with the permanence of death affects their reaction to a euthanasia in the period immediately after it occurs. While I wouldn't say they are necessarily more quick to recover from a pet's death, they appear to me to regain focus on the future without dwelling on the past and the loss of their pet. For instance, I euthanized a friend's pet last week, with five of her six children present. It was emotionally heart-wrenching, but it spared the patient further suffering. Children are resilient, and this family had plans to adopt another cat soon. My senior clients differ, as their pets are often the only companions they see, speak to, or touch for days or weeks. Not only does the loss of the pet devastate them, they are often reluctant to adopt another animal, fearing the pet will outlive them and be left in the care of someone else.

A pet may be a link to a lost loved one, the last remaining member of the "family." I simply *must* help them. When I make a house call to their home or assisted living facility, I find it hard to leave when I know they have few visitors.

I once received a voicemail from an elderly client named Virginia who described through tears that her dog, Sargeant, needed to be euthanized while she herself was hospitalized. I cried as I listened to the message, and I imagined Virginia in her home without her beloved dog there to keep her company. I lie in bed at night and worry about my senior clients like her. They have changed my life in unexpected ways. I truly wish I could stay with them for hours to hear their stories and do errands for them.

The relationship between the elderly and their pets underscores the importance of our four-legged companions in our lives. I attempt to educate senior clients and their families about contingency plans and encourage them to form a pet trust to give them peace of mind and help them form a viable plan before they adopt a cat or dog. I talk in more detail about this in Chapter 13.

When one elderly client, Jerry, lost his wife, his daughter Cara, who was also my client, lobbied her father to get a cat. Jerry, on blood thinners, was wary of living with a rambunctious kitten who might scratch him. He had similar arguments for each alternative suggestion Cara made.

Eventually, Jerry admitted his fear of dying or becoming too incapacitated to properly care for a pet. Collectively, we formulated a plan of care and consulted with their family lawyer to formulate a trust fund. We then found Cecilia, a four-year-old Ragdoll who was in need of a new home. Cecilia was a patient of mine, but the child in the home was allergic. Her family was relieved to know Cecilia was going to a loving home, and Cara was willing to step in as Cecilia's caretaker if her father became incapacitated.

Many senior clients need instructions clarified several times or even written down before we leave. Some don't follow my recommendations at all. While this can be frustrating, working with these pet parents is also rewarding and has unexpectedly affected me in wonderful ways. I have grown to love so many of them.

I've had to say goodbye to a handful of clients who have passed away, before or after their pets have also passed. A few are especially memorable.

HELEN AND BEAU

An ornery client named Helen lived with her shy cat, Beau. Helen was partially disabled. She had a few glaring personality traits that set the tone during her first phone call, when she left the following gravelly message: "This is Helen. Please call me at this number right away. It's about my cat."

As a rule, I do not pick up the phone unless I know who is on the other end of the line. My outgoing message requests that all callers leave a detailed message including their address so I can determine if they are in my practice area. I also advise clients to text me details, as texts are more easily checked while we are on the road.

From Helen's message, I guessed she didn't have a cell phone or an email contact. I felt forced to call her back right away so I could determine the severity of Beau's issues. Between house call appointments my assistant Natalie phoned Helen, who didn't answer. Natalie left a detailed voicemail, and we drove on to our next house call.

The "Helen phone tag syndrome" began then. I had an uncanny habit of calling Helen while she was in the bathroom. Due to her physical limitations, she was often too slow to get to the phone in time to answer the first call. That first time, she called back, confirmed that the situation was not urgent, and scheduled an appointment for the following week.

The day of the visit, Helen was irritable. I am ashamed to say this now, but early on she was so abrasive that I wanted to fire her as a client. She was so rude and obnoxious that I was amazed to learn she was a mother and had been married for decades. She ignored my instructions to confine Beau to a half bathroom. We moved furniture and stressed him by trapping him under a chair.

From a velvet electric recliner in the corner, Helen yelled at us the entire time. "Be careful, you're scaring him! Make sure you put my furniture back exactly where I had it!"

While I examined and vaccinated Beau, I asked repeatedly if he needed a nail trim. Helen insisted he didn't. We released him, and he returned to his secret spot under the couch.

The furniture was back in place and we were wrapping up the visit when Helen exclaimed, "What about his nails? I told you he needed his nails trimmed."

Natalie and I rolled our eyes in frustration, but Helen bullied us into a repeat of the entire process and we extricated Beau again. This time poor Beau was more "cat-atonic" and allowed us to easily catch him and trim his nails. I believe we, and he, thought the same thing. *Let's just get out of here and make her complaining go away!*

I hoped I had a full year until I next visited Beau. But just four months later, Beau had a cyst on his head. I drained it and recommended it be removed. Helen declined to do so, though I warned her it would refill with fluid, which it did the very next day. More angry discussions ensued. I told Helen that Beau needed to go to the veterinary hospital where I did surgeries and other procedures that I couldn't perform during home visits. Helen insisted I needed to be the one to take Beau to the hospital. She had it in her head that I had promised to take Beau to the hospital for any necessary procedures because she couldn't drive.

Aggravated, I said to Helen several times, "Why on earth

would I ever say that to you? I'm not a pet taxi. I have the number of a pet taxi if you need one."

Helen's family was either unable or unwilling to help her, and there were no friends or neighbors to assist. We managed to work it out, and Beau became cyst-free and disease-free . . . until he wasn't. I adored Beau and struggled with my relationship with Helen for three years. My staff and I all dreaded visits to Helen's. I didn't tell my assistants we were headed to her home until the day of, in fear they might call out sick to avoid her. Once Helen complained and told me to fire Natalie as Natalie struggled to retrieve Beau. I told Helen she was being ridiculous and gently reminded her that this repeated struggle to capture him could easily be avoided if she took my advice and confined him in a bathroom. On a subsequent visit I had a different assistant with me. Helen declared, "Great, you fired that other girl. I didn't like her at all."

One more incident between us culminated in a minor thaw in our icy relationship. Beau had lost weight and was drinking more water than usual. Helen complained because it meant more trips for her to empty the litter box. I convinced her to let me collect blood work. Beau was a senior cat, and his symptoms concerned me.

While we took the blood, Helen criticized us. "What's taking you so long? Don't you know what you're doing?" she complained. "You're hurting him!"

I wistfully longed for the days when I could take a patient back to the treatment area of the hospital for blood work, away from the watchful, worried gaze of the client.

At the end of the visit, I went through the itemized invoice with Helen. She complained about me and my prices but begrudgingly handed me a check. As I leaned over to take it from her, I accidentally pressed a button on the arm of her chair. The chair back lifted into the air and reclined.

Helen was now facing the ceiling. She yelled, "What are you doing?"

I apologized and pressed the button as fast as I could to return her to a sitting position, but it made her roll even farther back! She yelled again, but by then I had figured out how to return her to eye level. Helen was furious. I was inches away from her face when I started to laugh hysterically. I couldn't stop. Helen couldn't keep from laughing too. There was a fraction of a second before I fixed her chair when I considered leaving her staring at the ceiling, yelling and complaining. But that was the devil in me talking.

Thereafter, our relationship changed. I understood the difficult situation—one I would hate to be in myself. Helen was widowed and angry that her family lived far away. Beau was her whole life.

Blood work soon revealed that Beau was terminally ill. My conversations with Helen became more difficult as they were now about his quality of life.

At visits Helen now greeted me with, "Hi, hon."

Phone messages began with, "Hi, dear, it's Helen." Our calls became longer, and she expressed her genuine appreciation for my time.

I felt very guilty that it had taken me so long to connect with Helen. Meeting her catalyzed me into being more patient and understanding.

When I helped Helen say goodbye to Beau, she and I shared a long hug and cried together. As I wrapped Beau and started to leave, Helen realized this would be the last time we would see each other. I encouraged her to adopt another cat and suggested a pet trust and plan should she pass before him or her. She sighed and said that Beau would be her last pet. It was a much harder parting than I ever expected when we first met.

COLLETTE AND CHAMINOU

I had a lovely client named Collette who lived in a memory nursing unit with her cat, Chaminou. They came into my life through one of Collette's nurses, Kathie, another client of mine. Kathie was Collette's guardian angel and my co-conspirator in Chaminou's care and my plot to keep him in Collette's company.

Collette shared her personal story each time I visited. She had moved to the United States from France decades earlier with her husband. Unfortunately, she no longer had any immediate family members who were alive. It broke my heart to hear her recount how her son suffered and later died of cancer.

Not all of Collette's stories were sad. For instance, she greeted us every time with the same joke about Chaminou. She said he spoke three languages: English, French, and cat! We always laughed as if it was the first time we'd heard the joke and it was the funniest joke ever told.

Chaminou had some gastrointestinal ailments that occasionally required laxative treatments. The nursing home allowed cats but had strict rules against residents keeping pet medication in their rooms. Collette's memory issues made it a valid concern. She might become confused and accidentally self-medicate. We devised a plan to have Kathie treat Chaminou on her shifts.

With time, Collette's memory deteriorated, and Chaminou's health declined. He was an elderly patient and developed chronic renal failure. Treatment now involved more medication, diet changes, and occasional fluid administration. Together, Kathie and I did all we could to keep him stable.

When Chaminou's health status became terminal, we faced the impossibility of deciding how to approach Collette with the bad news. Her memory issues meant she forgot entire conversations we had about his disease. She was easily agitated. At one visit she accused a nurse of stealing her wallet, which we located minutes later in a purse hidden deep within Collette's closet.

A few times Collette called me in tears to relay episodes when Chaminou was too weak to get up to eat. We visited her and discussed that he was dying. She understood, cried, and seemed lucid. Yet the following week, it was as if the conversation had never happened. It was painful to revisit the diagnosis with her repeatedly and see her visibly crumble with the "new" reality.

My biggest concern was that Chaminou might die with only Collette there. Kathie and I felt that it would be best to intervene and humanely euthanize Chaminou so Collette could be there to witness it and hopefully not find herself, weeks later, frantically in search of him after he had passed. We needed to be sure she comprehended the situation. But Collette seemed to be in physical decline too. I feared what would happen to her without her best friend's company.

The day ultimately arrived and Natalie, Kathie, and I dragged our distraught selves into Collette's room. We gently and respectfully sedated Chaminou and then administered the final medication. Collette understood what was happening. She wanted to spare Chaminou from becoming worse or dying in her presence. It was incredibly difficult for all of us.

When Chaminou had passed peacefully, Natalie, who spoke French, whispered to Collette what translated to, "Alas, he is gone."

Collette quietly sobbed with us for several minutes.

For weeks, I cried every time I drove by Collette's building. I am tearful now as I remember it. I continued to communicate with Kathie for a month to check on how Collette took the loss. She was confused at first but soon understood, remembering our visit and the cat's death.

Sadly, as I feared, Collette passed away three months after our visit. I find peace and comfort when I picture them all together—Collette with her son, husband, and of course, Chaminou.

GEORGIA AND JUNIOR (JUNEY)

Georgia was a lovely elderly client who lived with her cat, Juney (Georgia Junior). Georgia liked to play the part of curmudgeon, and I loved this about her, but I saw through her immediately. I was also fond of them because I loved the name Georgia enough to name my own dog Georgia. Juney went outdoors and suffered various injuries getting into neighborhood cat fights. I saw her more often than I might have needed to had she been an exclusively indoor cat. Juney was, as Georgia phrased it, "Living her best life." I wasn't in complete agreement.

I looked forward to catching a glimpse of Georgia through her dining room window whenever we arrived for an appointment. She always sat with her chair facing outside as she waited for us. She tapped on the window and pointed toward the front door, our cue to let ourselves in. She then gestured toward the refrigerator, where I would find the remains of the antibiotics I had prescribed for Juney at the last visit, only half-used and long expired. When I gently reprimanded Georgia, she'd wink at me and tell me to "Shut the hell up, you pain in the a**."

Georgia had bowls of M&M's all over the house. She instructed Natalie and me to eat them, another reason I looked forward to our visits. She reminded me of my grandfather, who always kept root beer candy in his pockets. I didn't like root beer but ate them anyway. I felt the same way about Georgia's requests.

Georgia was a crossword puzzle lover, like me. Some days I sat at her table and peeked at her unfinished puzzles. I liked to tease her about a wrong answer. She always said I was too young to know more than she did about crosswords, and life. We both enjoyed this back-and-forth, good-natured joking.

Most of the times I visited, Georgia's nurse Maisie was present. Maisie eventually became a client of mine as well. She gave me updates on Georgia and Juney when I saw her kitty, Bob (short for Bobcat).

One visit, I realized that Juney had a much more serious issue than a bite wound. She had developed a malignant tumor of her jaw. To properly treat it would involve surgery and chemotherapy, which was out of Georgia's budget. Given the advanced nature of the disease, we agreed to keep her comfortable until she showed signs of discomfort or loss of interest in her favorite things.

That day eventually arrived. We said a peaceful goodbye to Juney. It was more emotional for us, knowing Georgia had no plans to adopt another pet. As much as I tried to convince her to get another cat and a pet trust, Georgia refused. It was the last time I saw her.

But I had Maisie and Bob in my life, and she gave me regular updates on Georgia. For the next two years, Maisie handed me a Christmas card from Georgia. I still have them and cherish them.

CHAPTER 13

PET TRUSTS

Karl Lagerfeld made headlines in 2019 when he died and left much of his estate, valued between $195 and $300 million, to his cat, a Birman named Choupette. That pales in comparison to the world's richest pet, a German shepherd named Gunther IV, who inherited assets worth $370 million. The money was passed down through canine generations after being left to the original Gunther when German countess Carlotta Liebenstein died in 1991.

What is important about these pets is that they are foreigners. Here in the US, pets are considered property and you can't legally leave one type of property to another type. Even in France, it's illegal to name an animal as an heir in a will, but Mr. Lagerfeld got around the laws by creating a foundation in Choupette's name. Pet trusts are a valid legal option for leaving funds to animals. Many of my elderly clients are anxious about who will care for their beloved dogs and cats if they are unable to do so. They're relieved to learn about the different options.

I have a few patients who were adopted into wonderful new forever homes after their previous owners died. But these stories are the exception, not the rule. While no one likes to think about the subject of wills and aftercare of their pets in the event of their death, between five and seven million pets enter animal shelters each year in the United States because their pet parents passed away without making provisions for them. It's not as easy as you might think to make pet care arrangements. Pets are treated as property in the event of a death. There are several sources you can enlist to assist with a personal directive. But it's not as simple as stating in a will, "I want my dogs to be taken care of," or "My cat should go to my nephew Michael." This type of informal arrangement, also known as either a written or oral agreement, is cost-free when written into a will but not enforceable. There is always the possibility the person listed may be unwilling or not financially able to properly care for the pet.

If you already have a will, a lawyer can easily and inexpensively draw up addenda. A Letter of Instruction is one such supplement. A Pet Protection Agreement is a slightly more enforceable document. Terms may vary slightly from state to state. The Pet Protection Agreement includes many of the details in a pet trust (which I prefer and will discuss shortly) and requires a designated guardian's signature. Most agreements are valid for the life of the pet or twenty-one years, whichever comes first.

Some lawyers may also recommend a third option, known as a limited durable power of attorney. It dictates who makes animal care decisions while the pet owners are still alive. Because it is not permanent, I generally don't recommend it.

While these options are easier to draw up than a pet trust, the main problem is that wills are not typically enforced the same day or week after someone dies, so these wishes are not always honored. A clear pet plan established beforehand can help avoid the tragic euthanasia of a pet when provisions aren't located in time.

Resources such as the book *PerPETual Care: Who Will Look After Your Pets If You're Not Around?* by Lisa Rogak outline the process. Rogak discusses how to avoid challenges from relatives who don't want to be burdened with a pet and gives clear and effective advice for making legal plans.

I also recommend you refer to www.aspca.org. The organization has many helpful tips and specific information to include in documents to ensure a smooth transition when the time comes.

You can also draw up a contract that includes financial arrangements with your veterinarian for future pet care. Ideally, you should also discuss this with your lawyer.

Another option is to purchase pet health insurance and designate funds to maintain the policy after your death to assist in the pet's future medical expenses.

The option I recommend most is to form a pet trust. Pet trusts are documents set up to list clear, detailed arrangements for the pet's care after the pet parent has passed away. There are three types. Refer to this link to follow your specific state's law:

www.aspca.org/pet-care/pet-planning/pet-trust-laws

The cost to have an attorney draw one up, which could be thousands of dollars, is outweighed by the benefits. These trusts help to reduce probate tax (the so-called "death tax"). Several states have pet trust laws in place, and they are considered legal in all fifty states.

TRADITIONAL PET TRUSTS

I recommend a traditional pet trust. It gives you a great deal of control over your pet's care. The key decisions you will need to make are:

- Who will handle the finances for your pet? (trustee)
- Who will be the new owner? (caretaker/beneficiary)
- What expenses will the trustee reimburse to the caretaker?
- What type of care will your pet receive? (List specific instructions for feeding, amount of food per meal, housing, veterinary care, and amount of exercise.)

- What will happen in the event the caretaker can no longer keep your pet?

It is helpful to list alternate caretakers in case that occurs. People's situations can change years after the trust is made, so planning for conceivable scenarios is best.

Below is a sample of language to be added to legal documents, provided by the Humane Society of the United States. Its verbiage grants broad discretion to the executor in making decisions about your pet and in expending funds on the animal's behalf. It also makes clear what to do in the time period immediately after death, before the permanent pet placement can occur, if there are delays in the transfer for any reason.

> {Article Number} A. As a matter of high priority and importance, I direct my Personal Representative to place any and all animals I may own at the time of my death with another individual or family (that is, in a private, noninstitutionalized setting) where such animals will be cared for in a manner that any responsible, devoted pet owner would afford to his or her pets. Prior to initiating such efforts to place my animals, I direct my Personal Representative to consult _____ DVM/VMD (currently at the _____ Hospital), or, in the event of Dr. _____ 's unavailability, a veterinarian chosen by my Personal Representative, to ensure that each animal is in generally good health and is not suffering physically. In addition, I direct my Personal Representative to provide any needed reasonable veterinary care that my animal(s) may need at that time to restore the animal(s) to generally good health and to alleviate suffering, if possible. Any animal(s) not in generally good health or who is so suffering—and whose care is beyond the capabilities

of veterinary medicine, reasonably employed, to restore to generally good health or to alleviate suffering—shall be euthanized, cremated, and the ashes disposed of at the discretion of my Personal Representative. Any expenses incurred for the care (including the costs of veterinary services), placement, or transportation of my animals, or to otherwise effect the purposes of this Article _____ up to the time of placement, shall be charged against the principal of my residuary estate. Decisions my Personal Representative makes under this Article _____—for example, with respect to the veterinary care to be afforded to my animal(s) and the costs of such care—shall be final. My intention is that my Personal Representative have the broadest possible discretion to carry out the purposes of this paragraph.

Additionally, it is important to find two responsible friends or relatives to serve as temporary emergency caregivers to step in and help until the permanent arrangements can be implemented. They should have a copy of your keys, plus care and feeding instructions, and your veterinarian's contact information. You should post removable "in case of emergency" notices on front and back doors and windows, with the specific number and type of pets in the house. Do not use stickers, as they can be difficult to remove in a hurry.

STATUTORY/HONORARY PET TRUST

There are two other types of pet trusts, both less costly but also less comprehensive. The first is a statutory or honorary pet trust. It is in effect while you are alive, as well as upon your death, and it controls how your designated funds are disbursed. It may provide more flexibility than a traditional trust and is the simplest to arrange, particularly if you already know who your pet's caretaker will be. You must first verify that the person is aware of your wishes and agrees to perform them. Most, but not all, states recognize statutory pet trusts, yet unfortunately they are not always enforced by the courts.

REVOCABLE LIVING TRUST

The other trust option is a revocable living trust, which avoids probate taxation after death. It can eliminate the majority of disputes and challenges to a standard will. While legal challenges to trusts are very rare, they do occur.

Many of us remember the famous case of Leona Helmsley. She allocated $12 million for the care of her pets, and her heirs challenged her wishes. They succeeded in reducing that amount to $2 million. A properly drawn-up trust will protect against an unfortunate outcome such as this. Further resources on the subject can be found at http://www.nolo.com.

If you do not prepare legal documents for pet care, your pets will automatically go to your residuary beneficiary—the person or persons who will receive everything not specifically assigned in your final legal documents. If you don't have a will or trust in place, your pet will go to your next of kin.

OTHER OPTIONS

If there is no one you'd feel comfortable leaving your pet's care to, there are a few other options to consider to help prevent a situation in which your pet is relinquished to a shelter. Fostering can provide a temporary home until a new owner can be found. You may arrange this with your breeder or the shelter from which you originally adopted your pet. You may also contact a breed-specific rescue organization you trust, a local animal shelter, or your veterinarian, to help.

Another lesser-known option is offered by some veterinary colleges. They provide legacy/bequest services for pets. In a legacy service, a veterinary student adopts your pet and cares for him or her for the rest of the pet's life. Funding for future pet care can come from cash, stocks, bonds, annuities, and assets such as your home or car. There are various ways to make those funds accessible. A living trust allows you to transfer cash or other assets into the designated fund while you are alive. You may also name your pet trust as a beneficiary in your life insurance policy. This is best discussed with an attorney or qualified financial adviser.

The Humane Society of the United States has a Humane Legacy program that can help you to contribute money toward future care of your pet. You may make bequests to be used for others as well through their planned giving office. (1-800-808-7858, www. legacy.humanesociety.org/humane-legacy-society)

Check the local humane society and other shelters for similar programs. Hopalong (www.hopalong.org) is one of many second-chance animal rescue groups. Hopalong's Pet Survivor Program (PSP) rehomes pets and ensures they won't end up in a shelter. They accept pets regardless of age or health status. But it is costly and requires a minimum donation of $10,000 from the pet owners.

Another national program I often recommend, called Pet Peace of Mind, is dedicated to helping seriously ill pet parents maintain a relationship with their pets even as they endure end-of-life care. They have a volunteer network that helps place pets in new homes. They are in forty-three states and the District of Columbia. (www.petpeaceofmind.org)

I have advised several elderly clients to form a pet trust and assign a caregiver to enable them to adopt an animal from a rescue group. Generally, senior adoption applications for puppies and kittens are denied by such groups, given the pets' long life expectancies and fear the clients might pass away, resulting in those pets being returned to the agency. This reluctance to allow seniors to adopt young pets makes it even more challenging to match senior clients who live on their own with a companion pet.

I am often asked to advise in older pet adoptions, as many senior clients have medical conditions that require chronic medications, some of which put them at risk if they are bitten or scratched by a playful, rambunctious puppy or kitten. Slightly older cats with more established personalities are less of a risk in terms of energy level. Middle-aged smaller dogs can be easier to care for and are less likely to pull on a lead or otherwise risk physical harm to an elderly client. While many people think they will bond better with a younger pet, they are often pleasantly surprised at how soon they form close connections with an adult pet. Anyone who has ever rescued an adult dog or cat can vouch for this.

I have had several clients create trusts at my suggestion. A few have since passed away, and the family notified me of their death and consulted with me about aftercare of the pets.

I have also had a few clients pass away without a plan in place for their pet's care. It is more difficult to find care for older pets when pet parents pass away. Without a trust in place, family members will sometimes take on the care of the pet. More often, happy endings are less probable for the dog or cat, particularly if they are old.

EDNA AND BUFFY

Edna was an eighty-five-year-old woman living alone in a free-standing home with her schnoodle, Buffy. When I first met Edna, like my client Helen, she came across as the epitome of a curmudgeon, but with extra pepper and spunk. Buffy was a smaller beige version of Edna, but crankier, with snarling teeth she was always prepared to use on me. No one but Edna, I was told, liked Buffy, and Buffy liked no one but Edna.

As a rule, I am particularly fond of elderly curmudgeon clients. I see it as a personal challenge to crack their cantankerous shells. While I still worked in clinics, I was sometimes given a heads-up from a nurse assistant before I headed into an appointment with such a client. I'd stride in with my game face on, hearing the song "Centerfield" ("*Put me in, Coach, I'm ready to play*") in my head. I am stubborn and don't give up easily, so these appointments tended to last a while. Usually, by the end of the visit, I had cracked a joke or sparred with the client long enough to be rewarded with a smirk. Or I might get satisfaction months later, when the same client asked to see me again, even though they'd offered no hint that they liked a single thing about me at their initial visit.

I saw Edna as a challenge. The first time I stepped into her home, Buffy growled and lunged as Edna shared, "My damn daughter called you because the other idiotic vets couldn't figure out what was wrong with Buffy. I am so sick of being ripped off by veterinarians. I doubt you'll be any better."

I noticed a printed article in plain sight on her kitchen table titled, "How to Tell If Your Vet Is Ripping You Off," from a lovely blog known as www.sheknows.com. I took a deep breath, garnered my patience, and realized my years of yoga and meditation weren't all for naught.

Buffy, a senior pet, suffered from a chronic skin condition. She had arrived with it when Edna adopted her four years earlier. Unfortunately, Buffy had been medically undertreated, and I suspected she had a condition known as Cushing's disease. Proof of this diagnosis required a series of blood tests, all of which exceeded Edna's budget. My mention of it was met with chuckles and, "I knew you would want me to spend a lot of money. Let's just make her comfortable."

Buffy's ears also had an unpleasant odor, which I noticed as soon as I walked into the kitchen. This says a lot, as it was not masked by the stench of cigarette smoke permeating the entire house. Buffy had seasonal allergies and yeast infections in both ears, which were to blame for the horrible smell.

Edna and I came to an agreement: I would address the vaccines due at a later date when Buffy wasn't in need of skin and ear treatment. During my visits I cleaned and treated the ears and discussed regular medicated baths to further help Buffy.

Buffy's baths were an ordeal. She needed to be muzzled, and she kicked and grumbled the entire time. There was no way Edna could bathe her alone. When I inquired if her daughters might help, Edna laughed. She said they never visited, and disliked Buffy, so any help from them was out of the question.

I got a sideways glance of concern from my assistant Natalie when I suggested I might know someone able to help. I hoped Natalie could come alone and bathe Buffy to save Edna money, but I didn't dare make the offer until I made sure Natalie was on board. Based on the look on her face, I assumed her answer would be no, and I dropped the subject.

After the exam, bath, and a thorough ear cleaning, I applied a modern-day medical miracle ear treatment into each ear. I told Edna NOTHING would need to be done to Buffy for three weeks. No need to clean or reapply anything. Did I detect a smirk, if not a full smile, in return? I thought so.

I believe this turned the tide of our relationship. This and the fact that I was not put off by Buffy's behavior, got down to business, and stoically endured Edna's snarky barbs along the way. Also, it didn't hurt that the ear treatment wasn't only easy, it also worked.

We returned three weeks later to a much more comfortable Buffy, and a transformed Edna. We vaccinated Buffy and re-bathed her. This time Edna was much chattier. She shared details about her life. We learned she was not a widow as we had thought. Her husband had left her decades before, and she had raised their children on her own.

Edna was a tiny, frail woman, but I gained an appreciation of what her life must have been like. She came off as tough because she *was* tough. She also shared that she had lung cancer. A nurse visited every three weeks. The diagnosis came as no surprise, given the pervasive smell of cigarettes, but it still broke my heart to hear that Edna continued to smoke.

At the end of the visit, Natalie offered to come and bathe Buffy once or twice a week. She and Edna agreed upon a fee and exchanged numbers. I wanted to hug them both but knew our "second date" was a bit early to bring out my compulsive hugs. There would be many other visits, as we worked around Buffy's actual diagnosis for quite a while, because I was turned down each time I attempted to get the final blood tests.

I grew very fond of both Edna and Buffy. Every time I was there, the television played on full volume. We noticed Edna was losing weight and taking an increasing amount of medication, which eventually included an IV pole with fluids hooked up to her arm on a few visits. Her cancer had progressed, and she was in decline. On a few occasions we had to knock several times before she heard us; she'd fallen asleep and forgotten we were scheduled to come see Buffy those days. We began to let ourselves in after Edna shared where she hid her spare key. Once we came, did the visit, and left. Edna slept on the couch the entire time. We didn't have the heart to wake her. I left written instructions several times for her. Afterward she called to follow up on our visit.

Two trips stand out in my mind when I think of Edna. Once her nurse mentioned she had come to treat Edna and found her asleep with her glasses on. They were broken. The nurse quietly removed them, had them repaired, and returned them to Edna's head before she administered the day's medical treatment. God bless her.

Another was my last visit. Edna slept the entire time we were there, while hooked up to oxygen. Natalie and I both knew it would be the last time we'd see her. We gently gave her a hug, careful not to wake her, and left. We sobbed in the car afterward. I communicated with Edna's daughter a few weeks after the visit and learned that Edna had passed away and Buffy had been brought to a shelter. Without a pet trust and finances provided for Buffy's veterinary care, she was not deemed adoptable and was euthanized. It broke my heart to know Edna's daughters didn't take Buffy into their homes, as Edna had so hoped they would. Her biggest fear was she would pass away before Buffy.

LINDA AND BORIS

Linda was a long-term pet parent I saw at her assisted living facility. Linda lived in one building with Boris, her Chihuahua, while her husband, Edgar, lived in an adjacent building in the memory-assistance unit. Linda was a wonderful pet mom. She walked Boris five times a day, and he was unofficially co-parented by many people in her building's senior community.

During one of our visits, I was introduced to Charlotte, the daughter of another resident named Olga. After our conversation, Charlotte adopted two female Yorkshire terriers for Olga, named Marsha and Jan. I grew to love them, as did Boris. I now had three patients in the building.

A year later, Linda needed spinal surgery and could no longer care for Boris. She was unable to bend over and had a long period of physical rehabilitation after the surgery, with permanent lifting restrictions.

Luckily, she had taken my advice several years prior and made a pet trust plan. Initially, she had arranged for her daughter to adopt Boris in the event of her death. But after Marsha and Jan came into their lives, she changed the specifics of the trust and arranged for Charlotte and Olga to adopt and care for Boris. It worked out for everyone. Linda was able to visit him, Boris was happy with the arrangement, and I got to see all three of them. I continue to see them to this day. Linda pays for all of Boris's services, and her trust has funds set aside for when she passes away. Hopefully that will not be for a very long time.

I wish I had more stories that ended as Linda and Boris's did. Sadly, more end up like Edna and Buffy. The two vastly different outcomes drive home how crucial it is to have a concrete plan in place in the event that you cannot care for your pets, preferably with a pet trust or similar alternative arrangement. With a little planning, the peace of mind gained from having your pet's affairs in order is a priceless gift you can give to yourself, and them.

CHAPTER 14

WESTERN AND ALTERNATIVE MEDICINE

estern medicine has created lots of advances for our pets. Additionally, veterinarians have gradually become more knowledgeable about alternative medicines and more comfortable supplementing Western practices with them. As a result, we have more treatment options to offer pets and their families. During the last several years, I have come to rely on alternative medicine, both professionally and personally.

WESTERN MEDICAL ADVANCES

Veterinary medicine has largely caught up to human medicine. Digital radiographs are now the norm, and their sophistication far surpasses the limits of film X-rays—today, we can easily manipulate and share images between colleagues. Mainstream diagnostics like MRIs and CAT scans remain valuable standbys, but ultrasounds and digital radiography, including digital dental X-rays, are the standard of care for my patients now.

Beyond imaging, the array of options available now has revolutionized care for general practitioners like me. I can give dogs a monoclonal antibody treatment called Cytopoint for allergies.

I can give cats a monthly injection called Solensia for pain, and another injectable dog version called Librela. Kidney transplants are now an option for cats. Stem cell therapy is available for arthritis. Even prosthetic limbs, eyes, and testicles are available for pets. We can install pacemakers in their hearts and place artificial hips to extend their lives, pain-free. Vets now perform root canals and provide orthodontia (police and military dogs are often required to use their teeth in their line of work). Even laparoscopic surgery and cataract and lens replacement surgeries have become more common.

Not to mention, artificial insemination is not just for valuable racehorses anymore.

It is also not unusual for clients to have DNA analyses, the results of which have become more reliable, to determine the breeds of their rescued dogs. It is even possible to clone your pet.

Pet behaviorists are busier than ever, for several reasons. Rescued pet adoptions are increasing, in part due to the rising number of no-kill shelters. Therefore, many pets that have been given up to shelters, pets that may have once been euthanized due to behavioral issues or anxiety, are being rehomed in greater numbers.

Also, I have noticed that more pet parents are educating themselves about pet behavior, investing time and effort to train their pets, and medicating them if advised to. Much of society sees pets as family, and makes long-term emotional investments in them. Pet trainers and behaviorists are in demand, as families strive to provide the best physical and emotional well-being to their pets.

Medical treatment options such as oncology therapy and prescription pet diets to prevent and treat disease are more plentiful. Specialists, once only located in veterinary school teaching hospitals, have formed group specialty hospitals equipped with twenty-four-hour emergency services that are based in most major metropolitan areas. For decades I have referred patients to nearby veterinary cardiologists, neurologists, dentists, orthopedic and general surgeons, dermatologists, ophthalmologists, and reproductive specialists when necessary.

These medical advancements are amazing—and they also come with costs. Fortunately, there are several pet insurance companies to choose from. I advise clients to purchase a policy as soon as they bring home a dog or cat. They'll be in good company—a study by the Insurance Information Institute (www.iii.org) estimated 4.8 million pets were insured in the US in 2022 (Insurance Information Institute 2023). As with human insurance, preexisting conditions can prohibit coverage, and there are age limits after which you cannot become insured.

I have friends with two dogs who have two insurance policies for each pet. Some companies have wellness plans, others cover strictly Western medicine, while still others agree to compensate for Eastern medical therapies such as acupuncture.

If you plan to offer your pet all the veterinary medicine and technology available if and when needed, definitely look into insurance. One family told me that in 2002 they spent $60,000 on their ferrets. Those prices would probably be triple in today's economy.

ALTERNATIVE MEDICINE

Since we have become more globally connected, we have been exposed to medical paradigms of other cultures that challenge our traditional views of the body and health. Interest in exploring complementary and alternative therapies has continued to grow in the last few decades within the veterinary community, as evidenced by the formation of the American Holistic Veterinary Medical Association. While alternative practices are still controversial and not universally accepted, more of my colleagues are open to learning and trying therapies that do not replace conventional Western medicine but rather enhance it. Integrative, or holistic, medicine selectively incorporates elements of complementary and alternative medicine into comprehensive treatment plans alongside solidly orthodox methods of diagnosis and treatment.

What is the difference between holistic and allopathic (Western) medicine? Every vet who has a degree is trained in allopathic medicine, also known as Western, or conventional, veterinary medicine. It is sometimes referred to as "disease care," as opposed to the "health care" of holistic medicine.

The basis of holistic modalities is to stimulate the body's natural healing response. For example, homeopathy pairs cures with specific symptoms, whereas naturopathic treatments may help a broader range of patients, regardless of their condition.

Other forms are Chinese medicine, which includes acupuncture and acupressure; traditional Chinese medicine, which employs processed herbs; Ayurvedic medicine, which more often employs cooked, fresh, or dried herbs; nutritional supplements; laser therapy; and flower essence therapy or aromatherapy, which use plant material and plant-derived substances such as essential oils to improve physical, mental, and emotional well-being. (Please note I am intentionally not going into detail on any of these treatments, as there are experts in each field who could explain it far better than I can. My intent is to share what I have observed as veterinarians like myself have slowly incorporated these modalities into our practices. I refer to specialists when indicated, as I continue to study and learn more about these treatments myself.)

Hands-on modalities for both treating disease and supporting health include Reiki, which employs energy healing; chiropractic, which treats disease by addressing the musculoskeletal system; Rolfing, a structural integration of manipulation sessions; and Tellington TTouch ®, a gentle, relaxing method of touch created by animal expert Linda Tellington-Jones.

One regret I have in my career is not getting further training in acupuncture. It would have been the perfect complement to house calls, as so many of my patients are elderly and arthritic. Acupuncture, with its mysterious way of augmenting the body's ability to heal, can help with many other disease processes too. Combined with laser therapy, it has proven to be a game-changing alternative to surgical treatment of intervertebral disc disease in some patients.

There are veterinary chiropractors who focus more on the relationship of the nervous system to the spinal cord, correcting improper alignments. I know many veterinarians who routinely recommend patients to chiropractors, and personally I have had such great success with acupuncture that I tend to refer it more often. Still, I have had a few clients swear that chiropractic treatment helped their dogs.

Gradually, I have incorporated various types of alternative practices and treatments into my regimen. Faced with patients who are not responding to conventional medical therapies, or for whom surgery is not an option, I turn to these other modalities. Happily, what often begins as a last-ditch effort sometimes provides surprising positive results. The successes I have seen have converted me into a fan of therapies such as acupuncture, laser therapy, Reiki and acupressure, and Chinese herbs and mushrooms (Yunnan Baiyao and I'm-Yunity, respectively) for specific types of cancer. Now I regularly employ these ancillary healing approaches for their capacity to enhance my standard treatments. I can't always explain exactly how they work, but I recommend them because they do.

MODALITIES I USE: REIKI, ACUPUNCTURE, ACUPRESSURE, AND LASER

Acupuncture and acupressure: Relatively recently, veterinarians are catching on to the practice of acupuncture that the Chinese have used for 3,500 years. Depending on the specific discipline,

WESTERN AND ALTERNATIVE MEDICINE

points or channels are identified on the body to guide where to apply needles or place pressure to relieve pain, reduce inflammation, and help the body heal. Usually, the locations are found by palpation rather than referring to preset locations.

Laser and LED therapies are light-based modalities. They both deliver energy to a target tissue to precipitate a photochemical process known as photobiomodulation (PBMT). Both alleviate pain and inflammation, act as immunomodulators, promote wound healing, and cause tissue regeneration.

Light-emitting diodes (LEDs) utilize the red infrared spectrum of light. LED light is used for more superficial treatment such as back pain and wound healing.

Laser treatments employ wavelengths that go into deeper tissues. I used lasers for years to help expedite healing of bladders following surgery, and it is painless. Pets and pet parents must wear protective eye goggles during treatment. It can be combined with rehabilitation modalities such as underwater treadmill, ultrasound, and pulsed electromagnetic field therapy (PEMF), as well as exercises, stretching, massage, and manual acupressure and acupuncture therapy to restore function, alleviate pain, and improve quality of life.

Reiki is a form of energy healing that brings the patient's energy body into balance, enhancing the body's natural ability to heal. A Reiki practitioner is trained to act as a conduit for neutral energy that the body accesses for self-healing. Reiki reduces anxiety during exams and pain and improves patient well-being, particularly for those with chronic pain. It is a complement to acupressure, acupuncture, behavior modification treatments, chiropractic procedures, and flower essences.

I am trained as a Reiki Level One practitioner and employ it when appropriate for all of the reasons described above, especially with my hospice patients, many of whom I have managed treatments for over many years. I use it in an abbreviated version, focusing on specific areas, mainly around the head.

Prior to my training, I noticed that I was instinctually massaging and stroking areas, such as the Yin Tang point, an area at the top of the nose between the eyes (a key acupressure point used to reduce anxiety), and the GV20 point, at the top of the skull between the ears (a point for relieving pain). Training in Reiki helped explain why focusing on those areas quickly relaxed my patients, allowing me to finish my exam and treatment with a calmer pet. Sometimes I don't have the option to linger at the head, but when I can, I prefer to do it.

INDIA AND ACUPUNCTURE

In an earlier chapter, I mentioned the phenomenon of veterinarians and veterinary nurses adopting pets with laundry lists of ailments—we call it "Vet Pet Syndrome." Whether the universe has paired these pets with parents better equipped to address their maladies, or if it's just an excess of bad luck on the vet's part, more stuff seems to befall our pets. True to form, my dog India has gifted me not only with constant adoration and companionship but also with a series of illnesses and injuries that have challenged me both emotionally and medically.

India has mitral valve disease of her heart. As I mentioned, she has been doing well on medication for several years, enjoying an active lifestyle of daily walks and sometimes hikes in the scenic Arizona mountains. This summer she suddenly declined and became unable to make it down a city block without sitting or panting. She could no longer jump onto a couch or into the car. She was irritable and our family was alarmed.

Just prior to this, I attended several days of seminars on how to care for cardiac patients, how to recognize and treat the signs of advanced disease, and most important, how to realistically relay the prognoses of our patients. The cardiologist instructor explained that patients who receive a diagnosis of advanced cardiac disease are given an average prognosis of one year.

As I took in all of India's new symptoms, I lost all professional detachment and convinced myself she had progressed into congestive heart failure. Never mind that she didn't have a cough, a telltale symptom. I scheduled an echocardiogram to have her cardiologist evaluate her before I made any changes to her medical regime. But that meant waiting a month. I rested her and visited a veterinary colleague to get the blood work and radiographs necessary prior to her heart check.

When I explained her symptoms, he immediately pointed out that they were indicative of intervertebral disc disease. I was shocked at how I had assumed the worst, missing, in retrospect, obvious clues: India yelped and even tried to bite both me and my daughter when we lifted her.

We determined the locations together—cervical neck and mid-back—and started her on steroids and pain medications. Her radiographs showed no progression of heart disease, and her lungs were clear. This type of spinal injury often does not show up on regular radiographs, and did not in her case. We located them symptomatically.

Further testing, including an MRI while under anesthesia, would be necessary to confirm the diagnosis and extent of damage, but I decided to watch her response to medication first. If she was unable to stand or had loss of reflexes, indicating a need for immediate surgical intervention, I would do an MRI and surgery immediately. But her symptoms were not as severe, so I began with intense rest with medication, plus a watch-and-wait approach.

India improved slowly, considering that some family members inadvertently walked her a bit too far or long, causing relapses. By the time of her cardiology visit, she had regained energy and did not seem to be in pain, though she did make accommodations to avoid discomfort, such as waiting to be picked up to go in the car and avoiding going down stairs that she would have to later ascend. I arranged for the neurologist at the hospital to assess her. He gave me helpful suggestions about the likelihood that she would regain full or partial function of her hind limbs, with her left one being noticeably weaker.

Surgery was the only sure way to fix her, and her heart would be better now than in six months to a year, the cardiologist confirmed. It was good news that her heart disease was stable, but their comments made me feel guilty about not moving forward with surgery. We were to fly with her in two weeks, and while the vet specialists assured me India should be fine six days after surgery, I was convinced that surgery and then travel would be too much for her. Instead, I committed to medication changes and scheduled acupuncture visits at the clinic I worked at in Arizona, where I live half the year. I had recommended acupuncture to clients before, most of whom swore it worked wonders with their pets. Having never experienced it with my own pets, and not understanding it to the extent I did Western medicine, it wasn't the first therapy I tended to choose. Instead, I suggested it when conventional treatments failed the patient. But here I was, desperate and skeptical because nothing ever seemed to go smoothly with India.

Prior to the first acupuncture appointment, I began to wean India off her pain meds, especially steroids, which had more side effects. I held her for her first treatment and was surprised that she handled the needle placement well. Next, wires were clamped onto the needles. They were connected to a machine that sent electric current through the needles and into India's tissue. She was noticeably more sensitive to the spots where her back injury was located. While India was hooked to the electric current, we simultaneously moved the laser over the affected areas.

Within two days, India was perkier on her walks. I had not seen such a bounce in her step for months. A week later, we repeated her treatment, and she was noticeably less reactive to the needles. The following day, she tried to jump on the couch! My family was incredulous.

India has continued to improve and now gets treatments every three weeks. She is off her steroids, and has regained muscle mass and strength in her back legs. I am a true believer, and while I may not be able to explain it fully to clients, I have a personal anecdote, and India, to thank for making me a fervent advocate of acupuncture. This has resulted in multiple recommendations to friends and clients, who have also benefited. The combination of Eastern and Western medicine is sometimes the best thing for a patient, and they can work well together.

But how *does* it work, you ask? What I understand about acupuncture is that the needles function as a way for the healer to communicate with the body. Based on responses to the needle placement, the practitioner can find areas of pain, tensing, and reduced circulation. The Chinese medical technique, both for humans and animals, is to place needles in specific points to access the body's *qi* (pronounced "chee"), a life force that travels in meridians in the body, to help it heal. It establishes neuromuscular connections and helps with pain control. It can cause endorphin release, stimulation of circulation, and a decrease in inflammation.

Medical (or Western) acupuncture uses a series of needles to stimulate the body's systems. It is most often used after the diagnosis has been made by medical means, such as blood tests and radiographic or MRI findings. It is more often used to treat myofascial pain, by placing needles in trigger points, identified as tight, painful knots. Many acupuncturists use a combination of both types.

CLEO

In a twist of fate, I was asked to see a dachshund mix named Cleo, as a second opinion, just weeks after India's remarkable acupuncture cure. Cleo's owner, Ann, had been to her regular veterinarian for years, and they diagnosed intervertebral disc disease as the cause of her limping and mild fecal incontinence. She was started on a pain medication regimen similar to India's, and was making slow progress. Being part dachshund predisposed her to disc disease, as their long torsos and backs make dachshunds more likely to have these issues. Furthermore, the problems are compounded by extra weight. Cleo was, indeed, overweight and had wrenched her back jumping off the couch weeks before. Ann was told to have a neurological consult, as there was a risk of paralysis if this happened again. She left feeling guilty, mainly because the costs of an MRI and surgery were prohibitive.

Ann loved her dog and came to me at the perfect time. Fate brought us together. I prescribed the same acupuncture/laser/rest protocol India was using. Cleo responded well and lost weight very gradually. Weaning her off the steroids helped, as they can act as appetite stimulants. While I still don't completely understand acupuncture, I believe in it. It is never too late to teach an old dog new tricks . . . and in my case, never too late to teach an old veterinarian new medicine.

HERBS AND PLANT PRODUCTS

Client pressures have forced many vets to break out of their routines to include herbal medicine—herbs, nutrition, and nutraceuticals—even though our underlying knowledge of herbs varies widely. We keep doing it because the clinical successes keep coming. For example, I have been using pheromone scent-releasing devices such as Feliway (cats) and Adaptil (dogs) for relaxation and behavioral modification for years. Catnip, as previously discussed, has long been used as a mood-altering substance. Drugs such as digoxin, used for heart disease, mimic the actions of the active ingredient in a plant known as digitalis, or foxglove. It is a reminder that Western and Chinese medicine are not that far apart.

Veterinary herbal medicines include Western herbs, such as those used by Native American shamans, Ayurvedic herbs from India, and traditional Chinese herbs. Today's pharmaceuticals, such as digoxin, are typically developed by isolating or copying individual compounds. Herbalists, on the other hand, prefer using the whole plants, believing they provide a broad spectrum of desirable effects, perhaps because they contain vitamins and minerals that drugs do not. The synergy of the various components is key, and may allow lower amounts of the active pharmacological ingredient needed to be effective.

Cannabinoids such as CBD are arguably the most common examples of plant products used on humans and pets to produce medical and recreational effects. They have been used to help with pain, stress, seizures, and nausea, or to stimulate the appetite.

More recently, cannabidiolic acid (CBDA, the precursor of CBD) holds promise as a potential anti-inflammatory agent. It may play a role in fighting depression, as it has been shown to work on the 5-HT receptors in much the same way as commonly prescribed selective serotonin reuptake inhibitors (SSRIs) do.

Each summer, I give India a daily dose of CBD, combined with an herbal rescue remedy. I recommend it to clients for their dogs and cats during the stormy season, and during firework displays. I also give it when India is traveling by plane. This is not a substitute for prescription medication to manage generalized anxiety. But for these seasonal issues, along with the CBD, I alternate between my two favorite herbal remedies: Bach Rescue Remedy and Zylkene.

I use the Bach calming tincture, which is a combination of five flower essences: rockrose, clematis, impatiens, cherry plum, and star-of-Bethlehem. It is given as a liquid or a spray and is sold in various flower combinations to address stress and insomnia, to decrease unwanted barking, and to moderate obsessive behaviors such as compulsive grooming. I also gave it to my previous dog, Georgia, who suffered from a brain tumor at the end of her life. It was the only thing that helped her sleep through a night of thunder.

Zylkene contains alpha-casozepine, an ingredient derived from milk protein, which has calming properties. While not an herb, this over-the-counter treatment is an accessible alternative medicine in the supplement category, because it doesn't require the same level of stringent and time-consuming drug trials mandated for prescribed drugs. It is recommended to balance reactions to situational stress, such as travel, moving, adoption, grooming, meeting new people, and exposure to loud noises. I have recommended it for use during training periods, particularly for mildly anxious puppies, to help them more easily learn to socialize with other dogs and people. I also often suggest cat and dog clients give a capsule before a dinner party or loud gathering. I like that it does not need to be given for weeks ahead of time, and can be used as needed, lasting twenty-four hours.

JOEL'S MAGICAL ARTHRITIS PASTE

I had a wonderful patient named Joel. He was a handsome, dignified senior black Labrador who suffered from osteoarthritis. Many of my senior patients with arthritis benefit from a nutraceutical injection of Adequan that I routinely train clients to administer at home. It was a part of my regimen I depended on. Unfortunately, Joel had an unusual adverse reaction to Adequan injections.

Without it, Joel was at a disadvantage. We gave him thick orthopedic beds and installed an impressive ramp so he could easily scale the stairs to his yard, but we struggled to find the right combination of anti-inflammatory medications and pain-killers that would keep him comfortable without sedating him and taking away his personality and ability to fulfill his lust for life. That lust included his daily meetup with his girlfriend, Joan Jett, another black Lab who lived around the block.

Unfortunately, Joel was either in pain or acted "drunk," depending on his dosing. I was at a loss, and looked to the trusty *Manual of Natural Veterinary Medicine* handbook, written by Susan G. Wynn and Steve Marsden, and the Internet. I had heard anecdotal success stories about turmeric from friends. Turmeric is an herb in the ginger family with purported antioxidant and anti-inflammatory benefits. I located a recipe for a turmeric paste, and with some modifications for flavor and dosing, it proved to be the secret sauce that helped Joel return to doing the things that made him happy.

Here is the recipe and dose, with coconut oil substituted for medium-chain triglyceride (MCT) oil, which is too bitter. Ghee can also be used, but I found that more dogs liked the taste of coconut oil. All ingredients can be purchased at health food stores or on Amazon.com.

GOLDEN TURMERIC PASTE

½ cup organic turmeric powder

1 to 1-½ cups filtered or spring water

1-½ teaspoons freshly ground black pepper

½ cup coconut oil (There is some controversy here. Some say that coconut oil, ingested, can cause stomach upset in dogs, but it has not been my experience.)

When mixed in a pan on low heat, the paste should become a slightly thick slurry (not watery). It can be stored in a jar with a lid in the fridge for up to two weeks.

Dosing: either directly into the dog food or mixed with water, bone broth, or kefir, divided into two doses if dogs are fed twice daily, because the half-life effectiveness is not long.

Small dogs should start with about ¼ teaspoon per day, medium dogs ½ teaspoon per day, large dogs start at ¾ teaspoon per day, and giant dogs 1 teaspoon. An easy way to think about it is ⅛ to ¼ teaspoon per day for every ten pounds of weight (e.g., ½ to 1 teaspoon for a forty-pound dog).

I'M-YUNITY MUSHROOM AND YUNNAN BAIYAO

The I'm-Yunity mushroom, along with the Yunnan Baiyao herbal medicine formula, have changed the way I treat patients, mainly dogs, with an aggressive cancer known as hemangiosarcoma. It is a terrible disease, requiring invasive surgery and chemotherapy to stave off its spread and to prolong survival. It often presents at an advanced stage, with a patient collapsing or ill due to blood loss from a splenic abdominal tumor. I have come into many patients' lives at this point, sometimes after a splenectomy, and other times when they have opted not to have surgery or chemo. Before I incorporated this therapy into my treatment, the diagnosis was a death sentence—the prognosis was just months, or even just weeks, to live. Even the most miraculous responses prolonged lives from weeks to six months or a year.

One patient of mine, Dexter, was an elderly beagle with advanced heart disease. When he collapsed, his pet parents took him to the ER. Dexter had collapsed due to blood loss from tumors in his spleen and liver.

Immediately, I put him on both I'm-Yunity and Yunnan Baiyao. Over seven months later, he passed away . . . from heart failure. His family got to enjoy him for over six months more than expected, spoiling him the entire time.

I'm-Yunity is actually a capsule form of a preparation of

the *Coriolus versicolor* mushroom, known commonly as the Yunzhi mushroom. It has been used in Chinese medicine for more than two thousand years and is thought to contain some immune-boosting properties from its polysaccharopeptide (PSP) component. It's been found to delay metastasis. It is pricey, and there is a less expensive extract called turkey tail, which is said to be effective. I have only prescribed I'm-Yunity because of the remarkable results I've experienced firsthand.

Yunnan Baiyao is a traditional Chinese herbal formula used to promote blood stasis, or clotting, and control internal bleeding, which occurs with hemangiosarcoma. It has been shown to inhibit the reproduction of the cancer cell line. It was originally used in 1902—with direct application to help wound healing and oral administration for pain relief. It also stopped bleeding on the battlefield in 1938, which is how it became famous. It comes in a blister pack, with the central capsule being red and more highly concentrated, to be used in an emergency where there is a large amount of bleeding.

There is currently some controversy over whether the China-based company that produces the product has been adding to their proprietary list of herbal/plant-based ingredients a component derived from pangolin scales. (The pangolin is an endangered species.) There is another product available, from a US company called Golden Flower Chinese Herbs, whose San Qi Formula is "designed to replicate the actions" of Yunnan Baiyao. I have yet to prescribe it.

INDIA ... AGAIN

I now purchase Yunnan Baiyao and I'm-Yunity for India. With her latest diagnosis of subcutaneous hemangiosarcoma, she has helped me come full circle as a veterinarian, straddling the worlds of both conventional and alternative medicine. As my luck would have it, she has a rare form of the disease, which is aggressive, and does not have a hopeful diagnosis. As I write this, she is sitting beside me, patiently listening to me type, with a seven-inch-long incision along her chest.

But there is good news, and I am hopeful. I caught it early, and it does not appear to have spread. She required two surgeries within two weeks, first to remove the small mass that I thought benign, and then to return and remove wider margins, which are happily clear of tumor. It was her bad breath from tooth abscesses that forced me to anesthetize her to address her teeth and, since she was already in surgery, remove the latest in a long line of skin tags and benign sebaceous adenomas that she is prone to late in life.

But I was wrong; the tumor was not benign. In retrospect, her bad breath led to an early diagnosis and may very well have saved her life. At least it prolonged it significantly; if we had caught it much later, then we would have had far fewer options. We're set to try a course of chemotherapy, which is one drug that I hope she tolerates. If she does not, I will stop it and keep her comfortable and happy on her current course of medications for her heart disease and arthritis, and continue with her acupuncture treatments and LED therapy for her back injury. She will continue to eat her prescription diet for her delicate intestinal tract, as well as her glucosamine daily supplement for joint health.

All in all, India is a little dog with numerous health issues who resembles a cat with nine lives. She is on about life number seven, in my estimation. But she's strong, doesn't know any better, and is a good little patient.

Each dog is different and teaches us something unique; perhaps they are placed in our lives for that purpose. India has taught me much about unconditional love and made me a better vet by teaching me how to treat her, and by helping me be an example to other pet parents faced with similar decisions.

CHAPTER 15

EMERGENCIES

M ost veterinarians are a combination of different types of specialists: dermatologist, pediatrician, gerontologist, cardiologist, internist, surgeon, etc. Some vets specialize in emergency work. They are the thrill-seekers among us. While the rest of us don't seek out emergencies, they make their way to us nonetheless. Most emergencies are unavoidable. But some are frustratingly preventable. Dog-park altercations, for example, are an endless source of injuries, some life-threatening, many requiring surgery or hospitalization.

Many ER visits result from accidental poisonings. Others are caused by the ingestion of large bones, which can lodge in the throat or become trapped around the lower jaw, requiring removal.

Emergencies are defined by their urgency in my mind— emergencies are either medical situations that will get worse and harder to treat if too much time elapses before you see the vet, or situations that can cause death if left unaddressed.

While I am hardly the only veterinarian privy to off-the-wall pet stories, I have had more than my fair share as a house-call vet. Unlike a physician, whose patients are often cooperative and easy to communicate with, a veterinarian deals with a wild, or semi-wild, patient population. This is true of cats more so than dogs. It doesn't matter how domesticated our pets are; even if they wear clothing and are groomed, manicured, and hand-fed, they are still often fearful and, unable to communicate verbally, will over-react, jump, scream, and bite in response to the perceived threats coming from the hands of veterinarians like me. A cat can move quicker than anything I have seen on this earth. I have several scars to prove it. Fight-or-flight reactions typically happen at the most inopportune times. Our patients, and sometimes their owners, have short emotional fuses.

It's imperative to remain calm when called in to address an emergency, or when dealing with one as the pet parent, so you don't exacerbate the problem. I strive to educate owners to famil-iarize themselves with what is physiologically normal so they can better recognize when things are abnormal and warrant a vet call or visit. I also educate clients to understand the risks in everyday hazards—such as temperature extremes and foods and plants that are toxic to pets—and how to avoid them. Also, I stress that certain over-the-counter, not-veterinary-recommended flea and tick products have been known to cause neurological side effects, and describe symptoms signaling a problem requiring a visit to the vet sooner rather than later. I strongly caution about these risks in hopes of avoiding a "man-made" emergent situation at a later date.

RETRACTABLE LEASHES

But this was not yet the case when I experienced my own emer-gency at the hands of a flexi-leash, shared here in hopes of educating readers and preventing recurrences. In my case, I was the one injured. Yet countless dogs have come in for treatment with a wide range of abrasions, fractures, and sometimes death due to retractable dog leash mishaps. I realize the popularity of retractable leashes. But while these leashes are on many must-have and top-ten lists for dog parents, they reside in the number one spot on every veterinarian's list of most hated items. People have fought me on this for years, but it's true.

For the unfamiliar, the device consists of a long, thin cord on a fly wheel, much like a fisherman's reel. They range in length and size, and you select one based on your dog's size and weight. The longest extends to thirty feet. This is a top-selling feature; the claim is that you may allow your dog to roam and exercise up to thirty feet away from you while you can see them and they "remain under your control." By simply clicking the brake button with your thumb, you can rein them in a few feet at a time, as needed. Sounds marvelous in theory. The problem is . . . frankly, there are countless problems. I loathe these leashes. Here's why.

The leashes teach a dog to pull. A dog wants to walk faster than you, and with these leashes he can pull and you may respond by letting out the leash a foot or two. Now you have just rewarded him for an undesirable behavior (to pull on the lead) when you should be the helmsman of the route and set the pace of a walk. The reward leads to repetition of the behavior.

A dog ten feet away from you is not under control. If there is a scuffle with another dog, you will need to reel him in to be able to remove both of you from the situation. Yet things often happen before you can react in time, and both of you can get tangled in the line with another dog. Also, dogs have darted into traffic on a long lead and been hit by cars.

Several reports of finger amputations have resulted from people wrapping the cord around hands and digits. Think it can't happen? Think again. Has your dog ever sped off to chase a squirrel, deer, or another dog? Now imagine your index finger is wrapped in the leash at the time and how it would feel. If you're quick enough to let go of the leash, the weight of the reel and handle can drag along and "chase" your dog, who is now frightened and running away from the leash with you in desperate pursuit.

Human hands and doggie mouths and tongues are no match for a suddenly retracted leash. They can become trapped in the cord and injured. People and pets can be knocked down or pulled along the ground, which is exactly what happened to me. My head was turned one way when my ninety-pound Labrador got spooked and darted in the other direction. He unwound the full thirty feet of cord before my thumb could hit the brake button. By then it was too late, as I had already been sent airborne. I landed, face down, on the pavement, and was dragged another five feet until the momentum subsided.

This was thirty-three years ago, when I was much less wise, but thankfully my hips were more resistant to breakage. I sustained abrasions that started at my chin and continued down the entire length of my body. At first, I thought I had broken my arm, but thankfully I had not. Suffice it to say, I am not a fan of the device. I have been known to attempt to discard and replace flexileashes on the spot during exams.

IN THE ER

I attribute any skills I acquired in emergency medicine to the time I spent training in the ER at the Veterinary Hospital at the University of Pennsylvania (VHUP), now called the Matthew J. Ryan Veterinary Hospital. Located in the middle of a large city, with an enormous volume and variety of cases, it's arguably the busiest and most well-run veterinary ER in the world. An ER doctor there gave me the best advice: remind yourself you are not the reason for the patient's life-threatening emergency, and they would most certainly die if you weren't present to help. To this day I hear her voice in my head whenever I'm faced with a veterinary crisis.

I recalled her words during my first relief evening shift at a hospital where I wound up working for ten years. The clinic manager retold his version of that night to all employees who worked with me thereafter.

At this large, well-run, busy practice, a Siberian husky was triaged back to the treatment area after having been hit by a car. The staff converged upon the scene to assist before I knew their names. The husky's blood pressure plummeted and his veins collapsed, complicating attempts to administer fluids and lifesaving drugs.

Although I had a team of well-trained nurses, no one was able to place a catheter, and I wanted to place two. They had never seen someone do a cut-down to gain access for a catheter.

I was taught the procedure, which involves incising the skin to expose a vein, in the Penn ER. That night our patient was a dog who had fallen off an apartment building roof, where he was walked to save time going down flights of stairs. He came in dying, and the procedure helped save him. I never forgot him.

In veterinary school we were preached the mantra "Learn, do, teach." The catheter technique was a perfect example of how to implement this lesson. I learned the procedure in the ER, then did it myself the night with the husky, and I taught it to the nurse on the husky's second leg. He was stabilized and transferred to an ER and survived his injuries. The entire time I was eerily calm and earned not just a reputation for it but respect from the team. It was one of many moments I found myself grateful for my veterinary school training. To this day, the more internally stressed I am, the quieter and more composed I appear outwardly.

Another time, I arrived for my first relief shift at a different practice to an empty waiting room but heard yelling and crying coming from the office. The hospital's resident cat, Marmalade, had just collapsed. The doctor from the morning shift sobbed and wailed and was in no condition to treat Marmalade. I nudged her out of the way, introduced myself, and instructed the staff to assist me with CPR. Sadly, it was unsuccessful.

Everyone was emotionally attached to Marmalade, particularly the regular doctor, who wept inconsolably for several hours. I had to place her behind a closed door in a back office to muffle her crying so I could get to work. Someone drew a picture of Marmalade on the whiteboard in the treatment area, and it became a shrine to the lost kitty. I returned years later for some shifts to discover the Marmalade drawing was still there, preserved in memoriam.

ERR ON THE SIDE OF CAUTION

For every person who overreacts to a situation, there is an equal number of people who underreact to a medical condition. It's important for your vet to help you understand what's an emergency with your pets and how to act appropriately. Doctors prefer to address problems as they arise instead of on a Monday morning after they've escalated over the weekend. I was forever the doctor forced to work the unpopular Monday morning shift. I saw cases such as a Great Dane with heart disease who began to act ill on a Friday evening. Three days later, he was in critical condition, and I wondered what prompted the client to wait so long to come in.

A classic Monday complaint might be, "I noticed the blood on Saturday, but we had a baby shower to go to in the afternoon. We decided to wait until today." This was yet another situation that could have been easy to remedy that snowballed into a big problem over a weekend.

Several years ago, I taught a pet first-aid class at a community college. My focus was to teach pet parents to first recognize what was normal in their pets: heart rates, breathing rates, how to find a pulse, what color gums should be, and if a pet was hydrated properly. Then I taught what was not normal to help them distinguish between what could wait until the morning and what needed to be seen at an ER. At the time I ran the course, there were many excellent twenty-four-hour ER facilities within a twenty-five-mile radius of my practice and the college. This was my way to help put an end to bad Monday morning situations, for me and my colleagues.

Here are some tips from the course worth remembering.

EYES

Anything to do with eyes—squinting, tearing, and rubbing (especially with cats)—needs to be dealt with sooner rather than later. While some eye issues can be benign, others can escalate into a serious emergency in short order. "Err on the side of caution" will probably be inscribed on my gravestone since I've said it so many times during the course of my career.

BREATHING

Breathing abnormalities—faster breathing rate, open-mouthed breathing, large movements of the chest or abdomen while trying to breathe, or necks stuck out as pets suck in air laboriously—are cause for concern.

Also, remember dogs and cats don't sweat, and are at extra risk of overheating in cars or on walks. They must pant to release heat. If you have a bulldog (American, French, or any version), do not take them on long walks in the hot, humid months. It will probably not end well. I live adjacent to a park and am appalled when I see joggers in July with their French bulldogs alongside them. I want to stop them and provide a public service announcement. They clearly have not taken my class nor read my blog.

BLEEDING

It may seem silly for me to need to list this, but you would be surprised by what is misinterpreted as an "okay" amount of blood. If you have trimmed a nail too short or clipped a mat and there is a tiny bit of blood, it's an easy fix. If your dog got in a fight with a wild animal and is trailing blood through your home or you see red poke from the rectum or leg, get to an ER.

I had a client send a cell phone photo of her black dog with "something pink" sticking out from her belly. The Labrador had gotten in a fight with a deer in their yard. The patient was alert and calm, and the client wasn't overly concerned.

When I zoomed in on the photo, I was incredulous. More photos confirmed it was the dog's spleen protruding out of her abdomen through a six-inch-wide gash! The patient acted normally because she was in shock, enjoying the "golden hour" before the body registers pain and other serious fallout from injury.

The body will try to keep itself alive, until it can't anymore. If you have ever hurt yourself and didn't notice the pain until a while later, say, after you fell or cut your finger while you cooked dinner, it is similar. I instructed this client to hang up her cell phone and get to the closest emergency room as soon as possible—a rare example of helpful telemedicine.

There are many cases where the picture looks less impressive than the actual wound, or vice versa. If you find yourself in this situation, send many pictures to your vet taken at various angles. To help your vet to better appreciate the size or scale of a wound or rash, include a finger or ruler in the photo to provide a frame of reference.

Telemedicine came to the forefront out of necessity with COVID-19 and the need for socially distanced pet evaluations. I think it's here to stay, and it has pros and cons. When used correctly, it can be an effective tool to identify emergencies or to get prompt advice on how to decide if a visit is necessary.

TOXINS

I advise clients to induce vomiting of most toxins, preferably within the hour, with few exceptions. Those exceptions are important because certain chemicals or items do more damage being brought back up through the esophagus when pets could potentially aspirate them into their lungs, along with the vomitus. Mainly, it is easiest to remember that petroleum products should not be vomited up. If you are not sure what to do and cannot reach your veterinarian, call a poison control hotline or the helpline phone numbers included in most product packaging.

I also recommend clients make a list of contacts on their phone or on a magnet somewhere to easily access them when needed. Poison controls typically charge a consulting fee, but it is well worth it, if only for the peace of mind it may afford you. And it will be less than the expense of an extended hospital stay if your pet ingests something and does not vomit in time.

FOREIGN BODIES

Dogs and cats don't only eat drugs, foods that make them ill, or chemicals that can kill them. They eat things—objects that can lodge in their bodies, cause obstructions, and require surgical removal. We refer to them as "foreign bodies" because they are foreign to the body.

I have a personal list of the worst foreign bodies to avoid exposing your pets to, which are worth honorable mention: peach pits, Gorilla Glue, golf balls, sewing needles, string, yarn, rocks, socks, and underwear. They go down, but they don't always come back up.

Peach pits become lodged in the intestines, and even after surgical removal, patients are at risk of severe complications. Same goes for Gorilla Glue, which is ingested as a tasty liquid but forms a solid blockage that requires surgical removal of not just the glue plug but also the adjacent intestines.

This goes for most things that get stuck once they have made it past the stomach. Cats are notorious for ingesting string and yarn. It can become tethered under the tongue and then continue through the entire intestinal tract, pleated into an accordion-like jumble. It is a life-threatening situation. Often a client might notice a normally behaved kitty doing "something funny" with her mouth. If the client sees string, time is of the essence.

So many items—toys, balls, and bones—may have posed no problem to a pet for years, until they do. I have treated several middle-sized dogs who've choked on racquetballs. I hate and have an irrational fear of racquetballs. They are the perfect size to lodge into the pharynx—the opening in the back of the throat where the esophagus and trachea, or windpipe, originate and cross paths. This anatomical area is just about the exact width of the ball but is more squarely shaped and supported by small bones that form two triangular areas of open space above and below the ball that, fortunately, does not collapse and allows some air to flow. It buys us time until we can remove the ball. That small amount of airflow is crucial to prevent permanent brain damage from loss of oxygen, if you get to the vet ASAP and they remove the ball quickly. It's not easy. I have had to sedate many patients and use special forceps to grab a ball without pushing it farther back in the throat. Those cases were gratifying because within twenty minutes we went from chaos and terror to complete calm, with the dog resting comfortably as his sedation wore off. The families hugged me goodbye.

There are several videos circulating online showing veterinarians using an external extraction technique to remove tennis balls blocking dogs' airways. I don't recommend trying it at home, as the neck and throat area has many delicate bones that could be injured if the procedure is done incorrectly. I have not had reason to use this maneuver but don't doubt its effectiveness, and the advantage of not needing a sedative is obvious.

WHAT'S IN A NAME

Many of my patients are golden retrievers or Labrador retrievers. I lived with Labradors for more than twenty years. I am very familiar with their level of energy, ability to shed, and wonderful personalities. They are popular breeds for a reason. But they also have some common habits that require emergency trips to the veterinarian, including eating things they shouldn't.

Bailey, a golden retriever patient of mine, had been vomiting all day. This was caused by rocks he had eaten, which resulted in an obstruction in his intestines, requiring surgery. It was the third time he needed the procedure.

I have two other golden retriever patients, also named Bailey, who have needed similar surgeries to remove several golf balls and a key chain. Retrievers are overrepresented in the "dietary indiscretion" category. I have "retrieved" from Labradors and goldens corn cobs, Lego bricks, marbles, sewing needles lodged in the esophagus, and countless socks and underwear. I would never give the name Bailey to my own pet, for this reason.

The same goes for pets named Lucky, who in my experience seem to be noticeably unlucky. I will never forget a patient so named, whom I treated while I was in veterinary school. Lucky was a cocker spaniel whose pet parents left him in the care of their parents for the weekend. The grand-pup began to act lethargic, barely moved, and extended his neck out at an odd angle.

They came into the emergency service at Penn and made their way to the radiology department, where I was stationed that week. We were stunned to see a bright, long needle on the radiograph. Fluoroscopy, an imaging technique we used to watch chest movements in real time, revealed the tip of the needle had migrated through Lucky's esophagus and was millimeters away from puncturing the aorta, moving closer during each inhalation.

We moved Lucky to surgery so carefully we resembled a bomb squad gently relocating a ticking briefcase to a safer location.

DELICATE SITUATIONS

I once contacted a pet parent after surgery to share the good news that we had successfully removed her red thong panties from her dog's stomach. She became irate because she did not own red underwear.

By the time she arrived, hoping to get a closer look at the underwear, the staff at the clinic where I was working had mysteriously "lost" them. I explained that they might have been a different color when he originally ate them and then turned red while stuck in his stomach for days. This seemed to quiet her down, and hopefully it didn't become grounds for divorce.

It's always exciting to see what's actually in the belly, because sometimes we don't know from the history what we're looking at in radiographs, which only show outlines of objects. It gives us a two-dimensional view of a three-dimensional object. The guessing game that follows is one that has provided me with some fun X-rays to share with students when I give talks at schools. Golf balls are hands-down favorites for visual impact, as are bladder stones. They are obvious on X-rays, even to five-year-olds.

IS THERE SUCH A THING AS A PLANNED EMERGENCY?

Emergencies are obviously unplanned. Unfortunately, they arrive in a flurry of activity, often amid a busy day of appointments, with a reception area full of patients. In theory, there should never be a full waiting room because it means the doctor or doctors are behind schedule. But if you've been to a veterinary office, no doubt you've been asked to wait, regardless of your appointment time. If that's never happened, wonderful for you and your veterinarian.

Imagine the frustration as you wait to see the doctor, only to watch as a distraught person runs in with an unconscious dog or cat in their arms and is whisked back into the treatment area. Most clients understand the situation and express empathy once I make my way into the exam room to see their pet. Sometimes, though, the emergency is so dire and time-consuming the staff must reschedule appointments if there is only one doctor on duty. Otherwise, there's no other option but to wait out the delay.

I recall one night shift I worked as the only doctor (which was basically 75 percent of my career). A patient was brought in who had collapsed and ultimately died of heart failure. After I attended to the dog, I returned to the scheduled appointments after being forewarned that the next client had vocalized her unhappiness to the receptionist and all the clients in the waiting room.

I entered the room, apologized for the unavoidable delay, and explained that I'd had to perform CPR on the patient and that it was sadly unsuccessful. I hoped and imagined she might be a little more understanding, perhaps envisioning how she might feel if her dog collapsed.

She looked at me with wide eyes and was deeply apologetic. I have experienced this before, where a client is rude to the receptionist or the nurse and then perfectly polite with me, unaware that I've been fully informed of how she had mistreated the staff. But in this case, her response was enlightening.

"I would have never complained if I knew you were doing CPR! They told me you had to deal with a cardiac arrest." I'd never again assume that someone would know that a pet in cardiac arrest meant they needed CPR.

IT'S NEVER GOOD WHEN
THE FIRE DEPARTMENT ARRIVES

On another busy day, I was interrupted during an exam by my nurse Shari, along with a policeman, a fireman, and a bulldog named Winston. Winston was alert and wagged his tail at me. I learned he had fallen into a fifty-foot-deep manhole. Excited townspeople had gathered and witnessed the rescue.

Winston seemed unfazed. I could appreciate only the slightest bit of gimp in his gait. He had no clear limp, no trouble breathing, no bleeding, and no wounds. Once we cleaned up the grime, he appeared to be free of overt trouble. I remembered the "golden hour" effects of shock, and I didn't want to miss anything. The firemen were also insistent that we radiograph Winston to check for fractures not yet apparent. We radiographed each of his limbs, his chest, and his abdomen. Each X-ray was clear of abnormalities. Part of me thought they didn't want to walk out of that hospital without at least some problem I could bandage or medicate.

The biggest obstacle was the incredibly thick musculature that lined Winston's limbs. The normal measurements taken to set up an X-ray did not apply to him. It was harder than normal to see through his muscles. We needed to increase the settings to properly see the bones. All the while, Winston was wonderfully cooperative and a pleasure to work with, exhibiting no psychological aftereffects from his presumably terrifying experience.

In the end, I found nothing more than muscle bruising, and dispensed mild painkillers. I could only conclude Winston must have slid down that hole, and that his landing was cushioned by his muscles, preventing fractures that would have occurred in any other dog. Amazing.

FIRE EXPOSURE AND HEATSTROKE

In addition to my pet first-aid class, I have given talks to elementary through high school students, clients, and other groups about pet emergencies and pet care. I've taught pet CPR to veterinary staff, fire department volunteers, and first responders. While these personnel are well trained to treat people at the scene of a fire, they are rarely prepped for pet care. I've worked with groups to help them assist with an animal found at the scene of an accident or fire. Together we established a treatment plan with details of how to stabilize the patient prior to transfer to the nearest veterinary practice or emergency facility.

It is important to hydrate these pets because the increased breathing rate and effort can dehydrate them. Skin burns are also a source of fluid loss, and appropriate wet dressing bandages are key. Dogs and cats are susceptible to corneal ulcerations from heat and smoke exposure. Topical eye ointments, with or without antibiotics, can help prevent the formation of an ulcer.

Heatstroke can prove fatal quicker than most people realize. I will never forget one patient, a Swiss mountain dog named Wilfred, who I was called to see when the clients' regular mobile veterinarian was out of town. It was a steamy July day, with the temperature in the upper nineties at midday. I sped over to the house and was shocked to find Wilfred recumbent on the black tarred driveway with a tent propped over much of his body while a garden hose was being used to cool him off with ice-cold water. This was a very bad idea on their part.

Wilfred's pet parents explained that he had accompanied them on a long hike at a nearby park in the late morning. He had stopped frequently to rest. When they finally boosted him into the car and brought him home, he collapsed in the driveway, where he remained all day because he was too big for them to move him. They truly had no idea of the risks and did not call the vet for hours, believing they were helping Wilfred.

Appalled and in disbelief, I quickly placed two fluid lines and administered shock drugs. I sent the clients to knock on any neighbors' doors to help lift Wilfred into their car, with the help of blankets to hoist him up. I watched him decline in the few minutes I was there, and I knew survival was unlikely. The hot driveway worsened his symptoms, which proved fatal upon follow-up with the ER vets. Years later I still cannot drive past that house without the deeply saddening and traumatic memory of poor Wilfred and his senseless death.

A few years later, while driving around my neighborhood on another sweltering summer day, I noticed a house-call client of mine who happens to be an ER physician walking his French bulldog, Oliver. He was a few blocks from his home, and I pulled over to caution him about the heat. My words of warning weren't necessary. Oliver collapsed at his dad's feet. I told the client to get in my car, and we sped off to the emergency veterinary facility nearby. There wasn't much time to get oxygen to Oliver, whose already small airway was blocked.

Bulldogs are one type of brachycephalic breed at increased risk for heatstroke, because their ability to pant and breathe off excess heat is challenged by their stenotic nares (aka small nostrils), elongated soft palate (excess tissue along the roof of their mouth protrudes into the air circulation area) and hypoplastic trachea (windpipe that is narrower than normal).

This conformational predisposition created the perfect storm for Oliver. Happily, I arrived just in time and he survived without permanent damage or death, after a night in the ER in an oxygen cage.

My parting message: If you think it is an emergency, call your doctor. If they're not available, go to the closest ER. If you suspect a behavior isn't normal, call a professional and let them decide.

And at the risk of being repetitive: Err on the side of caution. It is better to overreact than underreact.

As with Oliver, choosing to go to the ER is much easier than facing the decision of whether to euthanize. Any veterinarian would rather stay up all night in the ICU fixing a problem than face having no option but to euthanize a patient.

Euthanasias are emotional experiences for all, regardless of the cause. Yet they are a part of every pet's short life, or they can be when we are given the opportunity to plan and intervene at the end of life to spare pets from inevitable suffering. It is arguably the single most important aspect of my profession to get right. Everyone who has ever had a pet remembers the goodbye, forever. It is emotional for the veterinarian as well. Whether it's done in the clinic or in the home, we strive to provide an environment that allows us to make it peaceful, painless, and a dignified tribute to a beloved pet. The next chapter discusses all aspects of the process and ways to make that difficult decision and handle the grief that follows.

CHAPTER 16

EUTHANASIAS

For years I've been interested in the benefits—emotional, social, and physical—of living with pets. The human-animal bond is unique. Our pets are not only our companions but truly members of our family. They love us unconditionally, as we do them. The passing of a pet is an emotional touchstone for those of us who have shared our lives with animals. For some it is as difficult as losing a loved one. The loss of a service animal is especially difficult. Their death leaves owners not just emotionally bereft but also with a loss of independence.

It can be devastating to lose a pet. Much of my house-call practice clientele consisted of families whose pets were in need of hospice and palliative care at the end of their lives. I would say half of my time was spent administering and teaching palliative care and outpatient monitoring of senior dogs and cats. I maintained a list of senior pets I checked on weekly who were near the end of their lives or struggling with chronic debilitating diseases.

It has been rewarding to enable families to care for their pets in the home in lieu of repeated visits to a hospital. Oncology patients and their caregiver families in need of regular monitoring and blood test updates often enlisted me to bridge the care their specialists provided. I collected samples in the home and forwarded the results and progress reports to their oncologists.

The longer I have treated the patient, the better equipped I am to help that pet's owners recognize signs of decline in their pets, and the easier it is to determine when treatments are no longer working. I strive to intervene at a time that spares patients further inevitable pain and suffering.

Because our pets' lives are so short, many of us may say good-bye to several of our animal companions over the years. Our final farewells remain in our memories, even decades later, as clearly as many other moments in the lives of the dog, cat, horse, ferret, and any other animal we lived with and loved. I haven't met anyone who doesn't recall in detail the emotions and moments associated with their pets' deaths.

I won't ever fully get over when my mother decided to euthanize my dog Zorba without first notifying me, while I was away at college. There was no emergency that made her decision urgent. Nor was she forced to make the decision by herself. Even without the advent of cell phones, it was possible, back then, for her to have reached out to me sometime during his progressive decline.

I mention it because I have retold the story to many clients who have asked for my advice on whether to involve their children in the decision to euthanize. I think empowering the entire family to play a role in the decision is helpful if the children are middle-school aged or older. Many home euthanasias include Zoom or FaceTime sessions with family members who otherwise cannot be physically present, such as adult children away at college or living in another city. There are many decisions to be made. A chance to weigh in on those choices is not just an opportunity to contribute to the final plan but also a way for family members to maintain a sense of control when so much else is out of their control.

It is not unusual for families to disagree about a course of action, and whether they should intervene humanely before their pet's body makes that decision for them. I have navigated this delicate dance of uniting a family at odds hundreds of times. It takes time to come to a course of action that everyone is at peace with, as we all arrive with our own separate life experiences influencing our decision. Families who don't agree are fragile, struggle emotionally, and try to think with their heads while their hearts cloud their thought process. I guide and encourage them to allow everyone to be heard.

During every euthanasia, my assistants and I relive our personal experiences of saying goodbye to our own pets. We have also grown to love so many of our patients, whom we have treated sometimes for years. Often, though, we have been referred exclusively for end-of-life hospice and euthanasia. Learning at this late time the specifics of the pet's medical condition often leads to long and heartbreaking conversations with their families. I must be convinced, before I enter the home, that the euthanasia is warranted. I spend much time studying the patient's prior records and am often contacted as a second or third opinion. Many clients have a change of heart once I arrive, which is understandable. I have turned down many calls to euthanize patients when, after a long conversation, I decided I was not comfortable enough to perform the procedure.

I had one terrible visit where I realized the client's description of the cat's condition was inaccurate, and his intent was to euthanize the patient so he could move out of the country. He did not want to arrange for an adoption as I suggested, and it led to a discussion resulting in denial of services while in the home. It was uncomfortable and upsetting.

After the incident, I no longer accepted requests for euthanasia if I was not previously familiar with the case. I have learned the emotional effects of being put in unfortunate positions places enormous stress on me and my staff.

Many families have expressed wishes that their pet would pass away on his or her own. Typically, this means more pain and distress for the animal. It is my role to make sure the pet parents make an informed decision. The families should understand the amount of physical and psychological discomfort their pet is in before they commit to a plan. I generally do not recommend letting nature take its course.

HOW TO DECIDE WHEN IT'S TIME

On several occasions I have been called into a home well past the time when intervention was indicated. To me, it is a tragedy to find a pet left with no dignity, teetering on the brink of a natural death.

It is a challenge to determine the right time. I send clients a quality-of-life questionnaire to obtain an objective score to help all involved make this difficult, subjective decision more easily. It is a tool a family can use to gauge the extent of pain or degree of quality of life lost.

I often ask, "How would you feel if you woke up and found that she/he had passed overnight?" If they would be relieved, then we move to the discussion of whether the pet is in pain.

The most common comment I hear is, "But he's eating. He must be okay." But pain levels and loss of interest in life are not demonstrated solely by loss of appetite. While the family may be convinced this is a good barometer by which to judge, I gently show them that a dog or cat who continues to eat is not necessarily free of emotional and physical pain.

"He's just old. That's why he's so thin," is another phrase I often hear that needs further clarification.

It is not my place nor role to judge. I often personally disagree with a treatment plan I believe will only prolong the inevitable, but I can only give my advice. If asked what I would do in the situation, I share what I believe I would do for the best interest of my pet. I often respond, "Just because we can do X (fill in specifics), doesn't mean we necessarily should."

I am there to offer every medical treatment option available for the pet. Ultimately, it is the pet parent's decision, separate from what I might choose to do in the same situation with my own pets. My job is to listen to their needs and ideas about what they truly want for their pet's last days or months. I attempt to clearly communicate what to look for—the symptoms and physical signals that indicate the end is near—and to intervene with euthanasia at the right time, if they express it as their wish.

Many times, I have told my own stories of loss, particularly if I believed it might help a family grappling with what to do. In addition to the story about my dog Zorba who passed while I was away at college, I tell the story of my most recent dog's passing. Georgia suffered from a brain tumor and increasingly frequent and severe seizures. Our family took one last trip with her to the beach and planned to euthanize her once we returned home. While at the beach, in full view of two of my children, she had a seizure at the top of a flight of stairs. She tumbled down, confused and terribly frightened. I am convinced I delayed her euthanasia too long by bringing her with us. I come to each euthanasia with the emotional baggage I carry and the regret that I waited too long with Georgia.

THE PROCEDURE

Once I am at a patient's home and we have decided to move forward, I let the client guide me to the specific place in the home or on the property the client has chosen for the procedure. At times, I have arrived and been greeted by large groups who formed a support circle for the family. I have watched them feed the patient a last meal and then move them to a bed, yard, lap, garden, picnic blanket on the lawn, tree house, or riverbank. One client lay down on her back and we placed her cat on her chest while I administered the final injection.

"Euthanasia" translates from Greek: *eu* means "good," and *thanatos* means "death." A good death. This is in contrast to what we call "dysthanasia," with *dys* translating into "bad." Dysthanasia refers to a rare abnormal reaction to the medication used in the euthanasia process. Dysthanasia may also refer to the period of time prior to the actual euthanasia, "the practice of prolonging the life of terminally ill animals and allowing suffering without palliative care or necessary euthanasia." This definition means an end-of-life experience without proper caregiver guidance and represents a lost opportunity to prevent neglect or provide proper veterinary care before death. It results from a breakdown of the system of communication between the client and veterinarian. That's why it's preferable to be proactive and to plan the procedure rather than to be reactive and respond to an emergency with a stressful, forced decision. Avoiding the latter scenario is the goal of every veterinarian.

I will only perform a euthanasia with a sedative prior to the second, final injection. Once, early in my career, the veterinary practice's policy did not allow me to administer a sedative prior to the injection. The patient howled loudly the entire time, and the clients and I left the room in tears. I will never forget how horrible I felt for them.

Sometimes patients take longer than anticipated to pass, which can be stressful and worsen the experience. But the sedative beforehand makes the procedure peaceful, smooth, and brief, and is especially important when we are in the client's home.

Typically, the sedative takes effect within ten minutes. Once the final injection is given (another sedative at a very high dose), the patient generally passes within one to two minutes, so it takes approximately twelve to fifteen minutes in total. It is important the family feels safe and supported as they observe the procedure. The pet should be free of pain, anxiety, or fear. This is where the home environment is an enormous advantage.

AFTERCARE OF THE PET

Making the decisions about aftercare of the body can be a way for the family to further come together. While many families are unable to bury their pet on their property, some are able to choose this option.

For the majority of my patients, I arrange a cremation. Most crematoriums offer two choices. The first is a group cremation process, where the pet is cremated along with other animals, and their ashes, or cremains, are buried at the pet cemetery on the property. The second option arranges for an individual, or private, cremation. The animal's cremains are sent to the client in a wooden box with a brass nameplate. It is also possible to attend the cremation to say goodbye before the procedure, then wait until it is over to leave. This gives additional closure to clients who choose to accompany their pets until the end.

Another choice of aftercare of the pet body is known as aquamation, a water-based alternative to flame-based cremation. The process is more established in Europe, for people and pets, and newer and less common in the United States. In aquamation, the body of the pet is placed in a stainless-steel tank filled with heated water, potassium hydroxide, and sodium hydroxide. Effectively, the process accelerates the natural breakdown of tissue, while it preserves the bones. The process takes twenty hours. The bones are then pulverized into a sand-like material that is sent to the family, much like cremains. It is a "green" method, and is said to be the most environmentally friendly way to care for a body after death. It uses one-twentieth of the energy needed for a flame-based cremation, and there are no toxic gaseous emissions.

Currently, aquamation is legal in eighteen states, including Oregon, Missouri, Minnesota, Maryland, Maine, Kansas, Illinois, Florida, Colorado, Georgia, Wyoming, Idaho, Nevada, California, and Utah. In certain states there are legal roadblocks because some wastewater treatment officials do not feel the process is sufficiently pure. I haven't arranged any aquamations because I do not live near a state with a facility.

Families vary in what they choose to do with the cremains of their pets. Some are held until the client also passes, with plans to have the cremains mixed with their own after their deaths or placed together in their coffins to travel into the afterlife together. Many choose to disperse the ashes on their property or in their pet's favorite places, such as the beach, a lake, or a dog park. Certain religions require the ashes be dispersed in a body of water.

I always offer to make a paw print impression memento while at the home. On occasion, I have arranged for jewelry remembrances to be made from the paw print or noseprint.

Specialized urns are available from various sources. Some families have requested taxidermy services for the pet's body or just the paws. Many arrange memorial services, while others set up funds to care for pets whose families are short on finances. Others make donations toward research in their pet's name, often to help find a cure for the disease the pet suffered from. A few clients have requested their pet's teeth, which was harder to arrange especially as a mobile vet, and I have not personally offered this service. Some families have even cloned their pets.

I have been involved in over two hundred home euthanasias and hundreds more in veterinary clinics. I've shared many emotional moments with clients. Some of them remain in my memory more than others, and the specifics are worth sharing.

HARLEY, THE GOLDEN RETRIEVER

Fifteen years ago, I worked part-time in a busy hospital in suburban Maryland. One Saturday, I heard a ruckus in the reception area and found two tall, bearded men in leather motorcycle gear carrying a collapsed, elderly golden retriever named Harley. They were frantic and sobbing, begging me to help. I brought them straight back to the treatment area. While I tried to determine the dog's vitals (if he was alive, his pulse, and severity of injuries), they told me what had occurred.

Both men were the closest friends of Harley's owner, who had died suddenly in a motorcycle accident. When they went to the home to support the grieving family, one of them accidentally drove over Harley, who was napping on the driveway. Poor Harley was very old, could barely see, and was evidently deaf. He didn't hear them approach and didn't move. They were understandably distraught and inconsolable. They pleaded with me to save Harley, and I promised to do all I could. Sadly, I discovered a large, ruptured tumor in Harley's abdomen in addition to the already fragile, arthritic hips, which were now broken. He was hemorrhaging internally and was fading before our eyes.

I needed to speak to Harley's mom, whom I tracked down as she drove to make funeral arrangements for her husband. Her two middle school–aged children were with her in the car. I informed her of the situation, Harley's suffering, and the futility of attempting aggressive surgeries. We had already needed to perform CPR twice since he was brought in, and given the extent of his injuries I knew he would not survive on his own, or even make it through surgery. I asked for her verbal permission to humanely euthanize him. While she agreed with me, her children wailed and cried in the background and implored me and their mother to save Harley.

This poor family was so in shock from the loss of their father and husband that they couldn't process Harley's situation. I remained on the phone until the mother convinced her children that it was the best thing for Harley to be free of pain. They took solace in thinking it was his plan to leave along with their father and be together with him in heaven.

They decided to euthanize, with the condition that Harley's

cremains arrive in time to be placed in the coffin for the funeral a few days later. I promised to arrange an expedited cremation.

The moment I put the phone down I sobbed for several minutes, overcome with emotion. I was so terribly sorry for this family and what they were going through. I had been focused on remaining calm throughout the hour since Harley's arrival. Now I collapsed on the floor in mental and physical exhaustion.

I eventually composed myself and went to explain the situation to the two men. I suggested it may have been their friend's or Harley's final wish for the two to be together, which I hope and believe gave them some peace in the end.

BARNEY'S BUCKET LIST

Barney was a senior Gordon setter to whom I had grown emotionally attached. I met him as a puppy at a practice where I worked, and he became one of my first house-call patients. He was one of very few dogs who seemed to enjoy my visits. I chose to believe Barney intuitively knew I adored him and was there to keep him healthy.

Barney lived a charmed life. He accompanied his dad, Michael, on surfing trips. Although he never became comfortable riding on the board, he humored Michael and swam for most of the time they were in the ocean. And he faithfully ran alongside Michael on the snowshoe trail in the winter.

Barney loved long car rides and welcomed new adventures and meeting people. That included his new mom-to-be, Ashley, whom he grew to adore. He loved the extra hugs and attention he now received as a perk of the end of his dad's bachelorhood. Barney was even featured in Michael's elaborate surprise proposal video, wore the engagement ring on his collar, and helped seal the deal. I watched the video at a visit soon after the betrothal. Barney was also a grooms-dog at the marriage ceremony.

At eleven, Barney was diagnosed with an aggressive form of cancer that had already spread. His pet parents decided against surgery and chemotherapy.

Michael decided to spend some of their remaining time taking Barney on a wonderful trip to all of their favorite places. Barney's bucket list included a return road trip to Baja to surf and swim, and key stops along the way. They camped, hiked (the distances a bit shorter to accommodate Barney's declining level of endurance), and snacked their way across the United States and back. I received postcards from Texas, where Barney saw longhorn cattle, and from the Florida Panhandle, where they rented a boat for a day.

Back at home, all of Barney's closest dog and people friends spent time with him and spoiled him with his favorite treats. Grandma knitted him a scarf, which he wore for the last Christmas card photo they made with him. Barney was fawned upon by so many, and he loved them all back. I envied the days they were able to arrange and devote to this journey of love for him.

With time, medication used to ease the discomfort from his disease no longer worked as it had before. We'd all agreed beforehand to intervene to avoid any unnecessary suffering. Barney's home euthanasia was more of a ceremony; his send-off was unlike any other home visit I had participated in. I arrived after Barney had enjoyed his favorite meal of lasagna and Greenies. Grandma and several friends formed a circle around me as I administered the medication, and we peacefully said goodbye to Barney. I was sorry to have missed the funeral that followed, as I needed to bring Barney back with me to arrange his cremation. I later learned they all shared stories and videos of him and expressed how he touched each of their lives.

Barney was a dear patient. The highest honor I can think of was my nickname from his family—Aunt Dawn.

Barney's family inspired me to form a bucket list for my own dog. I hope to be in a position to plan, as they did, and be in control of when and how India goes. In the meantime, Barney's story reminds me to make the best of each day with India.

GRIEF SUPPORT

While I have a policy of no longer euthanizing regular patients of other veterinarians, I sometimes make exceptions. It's impossible not to when I listen to voicemail messages, spoken through tears, about dogs and cats suffering. I have played messages aloud to my family and shared with them why I simply can't say no. They agree, and I fill them in after I've met with the family because they, too, have become emotionally invested in the story. The emotional toll these euthanasias take on the family of a pet is obvious. But many may not realize the effect it has on us veterinarians.

Vets now have the highest rate of suicide of any profession compared to the general population (Brscic 2021). Many factors contribute to this statistic, including access to medication used to end one's life, in addition to dealing with euthanasia on a regular basis.

Compassion fatigue is a large contributor to the high rate of depression and results in mental and emotional exhaustion. We are repeatedly asked to end a life for medical reasons or for financial reasons if the client cannot afford proper veterinary care. The psychological impact can be significant, even more so on someone with preexisting mental illness.

The profession actively tries to address this problem. There are support groups, such as Not One More Vet (www.nomv. org), a forum enabling those at risk to seek out someone to listen to them and offer help before it is too late. Four Eyes Save Lives (#4EYESSAVELIVES) is another group hoping to make it more difficult to access the drugs often used in euthanasias from a veterinary clinic, with stricter control and protocols to monitor such medications.

Certainly, the grief a family experiences is greater than the veterinarian's, and we all try to gauge the distress level of the family in question. Some clients' grief is so extreme and worrisome that I counsel them toward resources to help after I have left the home. Follow-up phone calls can only help so much. The human-animal bond is strong and complex. The loss of a pet can signify a deeper loss than is initially evident, as in cases where the pet is the last remaining link to a lost spouse or loved one.

For clients with mental illness or other indications of extreme emotional attachments, I make recommendations for grief support. I determine what is appropriate, and within their comfort level. Many groups can be reached online, anonymously or not, or in person, if preferred. I give out fliers at the time of the euthanasia and provide clients with local and national resource information.

While our society places great value on pets, not everyone appreciates the grief process a pet parent goes through, which can make it difficult to share your feelings with family, friends, or coworkers who may not understand. It can be isolating and delay the grieving process. Mourning is and should be a time when an individual feels and expresses their sorrow over a loss, and the bereavement period varies with each individual. Dr. Elisabeth Kübler-Ross brought the subject of death and dying into the open with her book *On Death and Dying*. She identified the five stages of grief: denial, anger, depression, bargaining, and acceptance.

With pet loss and humane euthanasias of our pets, we sometimes see an additional stage: guilt. Pet parents may second-guess their decision to euthanize. This makes the conversations leading to euthanasia even more important—we want to ensure that the decision is made with as much confidence as possible.

In addition to grief support hotlines and brochures, I recommend several books aimed at both adults and children. Below you'll find information about books, local support groups, therapists, and links to sites to help you locate one nearest you or a loved one.

1. My personal favorite book, by a wonderful writer, explains and validates grief: *Going Home: Finding Peace When Pets Die*, by Jon Katz
2. *Smiling Through Your Tears: Anticipating Grief*, by Harriet Hodgson and Lois Krahn
3. *My Boy, Ben*, by David Wheaton

Books (children):

1. *When a Pet Dies*, by Fred Rogers, aka Mr. Rogers
2. *Being Brave for Bailey*, by Dr. Corey Gut (for children and adults)
3. *The Tenth Good Thing About Barney*, by Judith Viorst
4. *I'll Always Love You*, by Hans Wilhelm

Online resources:

1. Association for Pet Loss and Bereavement, http://www.aplb.org. APLB offers varied membership plans for families, with access to chat rooms to process pet loss with similar families, grief support/counseling, and webinars. Other levels provide pet portraits and memorials. Professional membership is also available, with guest speaker webinars and training for those interested in pet loss grief specialist training.
2. The Pet Loss Support Page, http://pet-loss.net. The Pet Loss Support Page offers information to those considering euthanasia of their pet, and resources to educate and support families after their pet has passed away. I often recommend this site to clients

for pre-loss bereavement support. They provide resources for pet loss hotlines as well.

3. Everlife Memorials, http://everlifememorials.com/pet-loss.htm. This is a wonderful site with helpful Q and A sections, links to articles and guides for grieving, and links to counselors and support groups by zip code. They also have information and contacts for pet grave markers or memorial pet service guidelines.

4. Hoofbeats in Heaven, http://hoofbeats-in-heaven.com/. While this is a site for horse loss, it provides information and guidance that can benefit all grieving pet parents.

SHIRLEY AND ARTHUR

I received a phone call from an elderly woman named Shirley that touched my heart. She contacted me during COVID-19 quarantine in early April 2020. Through tears she described how her elderly Chihuahua, Lola, was critically ill and should be euthanized. Lola suffered from a chronic disease that had been managed for some time by her regular veterinarian. Her vet practice did not provide an in-home service, particularly during COVID-19.

Shirley had broken her ankle a few weeks prior and got around in a wheelchair. Her husband, Arthur, suffered from terminal lung disease and was connected to an oxygen tank. It was impossible for them to travel to the vet's office. I could not deny their request and arranged to meet them on their patio, where we would euthanize Lola, contact-free.

Shirley greeted us with Lola on her lap. We could see into the home, where there were several signs displayed in each room: *Remember to reconnect your oxygen tube, Arthur.*

After we prepped and sedated Lola, Arthur came onto

the edge of the porch with Shirley, where he needed to be dis-connected from his oxygen for the procedure. He desperately wanted to hold Lola until she was fully sedated, and we obliged, of course. The entire time I worried about him as he gently sobbed, and we reminded him to reconnect his tubing once Lola had passed.

They were very grateful we could come. They also asked if we could take several cases of unopened dog food from their front porch. I donated it to a nearby rescue group. We also brought in their garbage cans, grabbed their mail, and left it on the porch.

When I reflect on this experience, I am grateful I was able to help this lovely couple in their time of need, in the extenuating circumstances during COVID-19.

ZIGGY STARDUST

Some patients and families have changed me forever. Ziggy, a fourteen-year-old Labrador retriever who was approximately thirty pounds overweight, was one of them. Ziggy had cancer, and I had helped manage his palliative hospice care for over six months. When it was clear that he was no longer responding to pain medication, we planned his home euthanasia. We prear-ranged with the crematorium to come pick up his body, because his weight far exceeded what I could lift with Natalie.

We arrived to find the entire family there, including both grandmothers and two children I had never met. It was an extremely emotional euthanasia, and we were all in tears. I had become attached to Ziggy. I often find myself unable to detach from the pets and families, making every euthanasia difficult for me. I am always sad when I wake up on the morning of a sched-uled euthanasia. Still, I was not aware of the extent of distress this family was in until several weeks later.

While the procedure was peaceful and without complications,

the crematorium service arrived nearly an hour late. I phoned them repeatedly, and when they finally arrived, I asked the family to wait in another part of the home while we wrapped and moved Ziggy. As we were taking him out on a stretcher, Natalie noticed that one of the sons was standing on the patio, watching through the glass doors.

A few weeks later, an acquaintance mentioned that one of the sons in Ziggy's family had passed away suddenly approximately two weeks after I had performed the euthanasia. I was devastated. I couldn't shake the idea that it had been the son watching us take Ziggy away. I felt even more terrible for the family and their loss.

I reached out to the mother and expressed my condolences and concerns that the delay in bringing Ziggy out was in part to blame. She explained that her son had suffered from long-term psychiatric issues exacerbated by struggles with addiction. She kindly thanked me for coming and shared that she felt that the day the family came together to say goodbye to Ziggy was the first time in years they had all united for a common reason, and it brought them comfort. Ziggy was her son's lifeline, without whom he lost his battle with his demons. She acknowledged they all knew Ziggy couldn't live forever. She hoped her son and the dog were together, both free of pain and suffering, in heaven. I hoped so as well. I never underestimate the role a pet serves in a family, particularly after my experience with this family.

Ziggy's story highlights the psychological benefits of living with pets. Many pets are the lifeline keeping someone with mental illness or drug addiction alive. Losing a pet, and along with it the steadying focus of responsibility of caring for the animal, sets up a vulnerable period, one when support is especially necessary. The responsibility of pet care has been linked to higher self-esteem, more social and extroverted interactions, and increased feelings of empathy (Jones 2019). It can also play a vital role in recovery from depression in young people (Brooks 2018).

Animals can provide distraction from symptoms such as hearing voices, ruminations, and suicidal thoughts. Pet interactions help patients manage their emotions and increase their self-worth (Wolynczyk-Gmaj 2021). Routine care of pets can give someone a feeling of control, imparting a sense of security in addition to companionship. The loss of that structure can be devastating to those who are struggling on a precarious psychiatric cliff.

ASHLEY, JEFF, AND BENITO MUSSOLINI

While euthanasias are somber events, I fondly remember a lovely experience with a couple named Ashley and Jeff. Their cat Benito (Mussolini) was twenty-one years old and in kidney failure. Benny had received supportive care for two years and began to fail in spite of it. I studied the prior veterinary records and we scheduled a time to euthanize Benny, two days before Halloween.

While I have seen many fabulous homes cleared of furniture to make room for mummies, witches, ghouls dangling from ropes, and life-sized grim reapers who carry bowls of candy, this couple had special effects one might see on Hollywood film sets.

I often schedule euthanasias at the end of the day to give as much time as needed to the grieving family. Upon arrival at dusk, I double-checked the address because the entire lawn and home were transformed into a cemetery. Given the reason for my visit, and the pending nightfall, it was a bit creepy. I drove through a faux-stone arch with a sign telling me I had reached "End of the Road Cemetery." There were about fifty gravestones with clever names and stories on them. They had one for each family member or friend, such as "Ashley, hung March 4, 1789, for train robbery." My favorite read "Geraldine Howard, a sorely missed mother-in-law, who was also an out-law." Disappointed I could not read the rest, I entered the home, more traditionally decorated but heavy on the skeleton-and-skull theme nonetheless.

Benny was a sweet, thin senior cat. Of course, he was black. The pet parents and I chatted about him, and I examined him, confirming their impression that he had lost most of his quality of life. We all agreed we didn't want him to suffer further.

The procedure was peaceful and went smoothly. I went back to my car to return supplies and give them some private time with Benny before I brought him back with me to my home office. This is one family that might have opted for a home burial, as they had their own home cemetery, but they chose to have him privately cremated.

I returned to find Ashley with her jewelry casting kit. She wore many pieces she had made, ranging from skull rings to beautiful floral pendants. She declined my offer of a paw print and instead started to make her own silver noseprint pendant and ring. This was a first for me. I had referred a handful of clients to a service that made pet remembrance jewelry for families but had never seen it done in person. Ashley made the nose mold and filled it with a silver powder, which would harden later after several processing steps. It was fascinating.

As we waited, they reminisced about Benny, beginning with his adoption. They had watched several videos starring him prior to my arrival. When they asked if I wanted to watch a bit, I agreed. I couldn't leave without Benny, so I had to wait for the silver mold to set on his nose. We watched home videos of Benny as a kitten, Benny dressed as Santa, Benny dressed as a pirate, and Benny as the ring bearer at their wedding. It was truly the "best" euthanasia experience possible because it was an uplifting celebration of the life of a much-loved cat.

After a euthanasia, I am compelled to give clients a big hug to convey my sympathy in the most natural way I know. With few exceptions, my hugs are welcomed. I see it not only as an opportunity to console them but also as a way to thank them for the honor of helping and sharing in the goodbye of their beloved pet.

With Ashley and Jeff, I hugged them with warmth and gratitude for what they shared with me about Benny so openly. I did not leave with the feeling I was simply brought there to perform a difficult procedure but rather that I had been welcomed into their lives for one special day. I got permission to come back and show my children their remarkable decorations, and they insisted I come every year. I have ever since, and will continue to do so, each Halloween.

It's not so unusual, actually—my relationships with clients whose pets I have euthanized don't necessarily end. Many times, I've gotten happier follow-up calls when they adopted a new pet after the loss. People cherish the memories of their beloved pets, and with the full realization that they will face loss in the future, they plunge headlong into new relationships, unable to imagine life without the unprecedented unique, joyful moments shared with animals.

These emotional highs and lows are daily in the life of a veterinarian. To further "drive" home the experience of being a mobile vet, the next chapter will take you along with us through some extraordinary days on the road. If there were to be a house-call vet movie, the next chapter would be the screenplay. Grab some popcorn and enjoy.

CHAPTER 17

LIFE ON THE ROAD DURING COVID

During COVID-19 my daily house calls changed drastically. For many months I saw barely any appointments, and only those patients who were critically ill. In the winter months, I saw many patients, mainly dogs, in garages and driveways to avoid contact.

In the summer months, we were back to more regularly scheduled visits, but with a twist. One particular week in July 2020 stands out. Hot weather was just one of the extra challenges we faced. That week held three days of appointments, a full moon on the horizon, and no shortage of eccentric clients.

It all started on Monday, a day I dreaded because I generally got a barrage of calls with problems that had arisen over the weekend. Both current clients and those wishing to be seen for the first time contacted me with issues that should have been addressed the week prior or over the weekend. Instead, most preferred to avoid an ER visit and waited to call me on Monday.

That day, four new clients left voicemails and texts requesting in-home euthanasias. My phone lines opened at 9:00 a.m., and all of these came in before 10:00. Two additional requests for euthanasias came from current clients. It took forty-five minutes to talk each of them through the decision and to finalize specifics.

Since we worked outdoors during COVID-19, I'd started making appointments in the early morning in an attempt to end before the full heat of the day made it uncomfortable. Masks and gloves were oppressively hot. We could not get back in my air-conditioned car fast enough.

On Mondays, I spent several hours preparing for the week's planned visits. We didn't have access to electricity in most garages, driveways, and yards, so to prepare for a visit, we had to anticipate any medication needed and count out the estimated doses, print labels, and craft write-ups of a projected treatment plan and fee for each patient. When the plan changed mid-exam, I relied on my cell phone to alter the invoice, if necessary. This prep saved us time at the visits.

I also prepared a list of each client's address, phone number, pet's prior weight, an itemized list of vaccines, and what else needed to be done to each patient—on paper. The list did not account for add-on emergencies, but it gave us a head start. I packed my car with everything I required for three solid days of appointments in the blisteringly hot summer sun. Barring last-minute schedule changes, I had a plan.

On Tuesday the forecast was for hot, humid weather with a chance of rain. I prayed for shade and no emergencies to lengthen the time we were out in the elements.

Our first patient, Callie, was a sweet, albeit neurotic, corgi who suffered from anxiety and displayed fear aggression. She was due for vaccinations, blood work to monitor her behavior medication for side effects, and allergy treatments. Her pet parent also suffered from anxiety, and it was clear she had projected her worries onto Callie. I've mentioned how many of my clients prefer a house-call vet because of their pets' neuroses. This was one of those situations.

The client was particularly concerned about having the visit during a pandemic, and had already rescheduled twice. We planned to communicate by text, which would have been fine if she had answered the texts in time, but she did not. Callie normally would have been handed off to us, muzzled, in the glass-enclosed porch where we worked. The southwest exposure and glass functioned as a greenhouse. Even in spring, it was a warm room.

It was already eighty-six degrees as we approached the space from the backyard. Then we found ourselves locked out of the enclosed porch. The patient stared at us through the glass as we attempted to open each door. I texted the predicament to the owner, whose response was a helpful, *OMG, OMG, I am about to cry. I don't think this is going to work. Callie is going to be so upset!*

From the kitchen her children stared at us, made peanut butter and jelly sandwiches, and walked away. I called the client to remind her that we were there, sweltering on the lawn and locked out, as I wiped my sweat-drenched face mask on my pants. She was upstairs in her bedroom, distraught and reluctant to even be on the same floor as us. She popped down, unlocked the door, and ran away, not to be seen again.

The exam and collection of blood was as smooth as it had ever been. I am convinced the absence of the client was key to Callie's calm demeanor that day. I removed her muzzle, gave her a little kiss, hurried to the Subaru, and cranked up the AC.

The following appointment went smoothly enough, as it was in a shaded driveway where we were greeted by a charming puppy named Koda. If my entire day was full of these visits, life would be easy. But it wasn't.

Our final appointment was with two large pit bulls. Jerry was aggressive and a minor sedative had proven ineffective. He required anesthesia to be examined or vaccinated. His brother, Kramer, was the opposite. He was overfriendly and normally exuberant when he greeted us. One day he had even pinned me to the wall with unmitigated joy when I arrived, and then he tried to mount me. Perched high on his back legs, Kramer stood taller than I did. It took two people to pry him off me. I think we may be considered legally married in three states after that day.

Our COVID-19 plan was to see them in their fenced-in backyard. The client made the mistake of having both dogs outside. Jerry ferociously dove at us through the chain-link fence, agitated and protective of his property. Kramer followed suit, completely out of character. They had been my patients for six years but had never seen me outdoors. I instructed the client to put Jerry in the house and enlisted the husband to bring out a box of treats and a leash.

Kramer was led out to a common grassed area adjacent to their home. Distracting him with food and taking him off his property worked wonders. Kramer relaxed and chomped away at cookies for the exam, blood test, and vaccines. It was a reminder of how dicey a territorial aggression situation can become. We headed home, exhausted after four hours exposed to the elements.

The next day, our first appointment began in a rain shower on a cooler morning of just seventy-three degrees. Conveniently, we were in a carport equipped with a picnic table. It was a smooth appointment—lovely clients, cream puff of a patient. I could not have asked for better.

Our second appointment was a backyard euthanasia on an unshaded patio. The client had not yet prepared the burial space for Benji, and it was a little unsettling to see her grandson digging when we arrived.

The procedure did not get off to a good start. I wouldn't call it a dysthanasia, but it was close. The patient lunged, growled, and jumped as expected and required a muzzle. I hate to muzzle for the initial muscular sedative injection, but it was unavoidable. I had prescribed an oral sedative to be given beforehand, but Benji bit the client when she attempted to do so, and then he spit out the pill. Benji needed an extra dose of sedative, delaying the process fifteen minutes. He reflexively leapt and yelped the entire time, which was awful. The rest of the procedure went without complications. By then the temperature had climbed to eighty-five degrees with 80 percent humidity.

What should have been our last appointment was Parker, a Chow mix with a history of aggression who had always urinated due to stress during our previous in-home visits. The client insisted we take off our shoes while in the house. Once previously, Parker had urinated on the linoleum as we held and examined her. We slipped, and my assistant Natalie fell and hit her head on the table leg. We both ended up with urine-soaked socks. Thereafter we instituted a "must wear shoes" policy.

Therefore we were relieved to meet the client on the partially shaded backyard deck. Still, the visit ended in a wrestling match as we trimmed Parker's nails. She got her muzzle off twice. The match was called at round two, with three of her four feet trimmed but all of our fingers and limbs intact. In the scuffle, Parker urinated on Natalie's shirt, which is hard for a female dog to do. We were done for the day . . . or so we thought.

I headed home, washed off from my day, and then drove to my first hair color appointment in several months, and since the start of COVID-19. Hooray! I dabbed on some perfume in case I'd missed a pet scent lurking in my hair and brought along some light reading. This was as close to a spa day as I would have for a while. After making a few quick phone calls to clients and checking voicemails, I'd have time to read and relax.

The first message was from someone I didn't recognize, with a cat who had been squinting for several days. This could have been an emergency, as it might indicate a corneal ulcer, which could escalate into a serious problem with alarming speed if left untreated. I responded that I was not taking new clients and recommended they consult someone else straightaway.

She said she already was a client. The records showed I had treated and euthanized her other cat, Mel, three years before, but I had never met the kitty in question. I agreed to schedule an appointment for the following morning, and made it clear the cat would need to be brought into an enclosed garage in a carrier. It was difficult enough to see dogs outside. Cats were close to impossible.

I had never met this cat, and therefore had no idea how nervous he was. I didn't want to go into the home or risk the kitty escaping from their yard. She explained she would be out of town, but her husband would help, although he had a work meeting at the time of the visit. I assured her I had examined many pets since COVID-19 while clients were on Zoom calls, etc., because of the social distance we maintained at the house calls. Electronic payment was common and efficient. If we arrived and he was unable to catch the cat, they would still be responsible for the house-call visit fee.

She confirmed and texted me the address, which I realized was at a bridal shop in a strip mall on a busy road. When I asked if she truly intended for her husband to bring a frightened, ailing cat in a carrier to a business meeting where he would hand off the cat to me, in a heat wave no less, and expect me to examine the cat in an open parking lot, she said, "Well, these are crazy, strange times, aren't they?"

Yes, they sure are, and no, I will not be able to see your cat tomorrow.

A second request was even more odd. Another prospective client shared how her husband wouldn't agree to have their male adult dog neutered. He was to be away for a week, and she hoped to have me neuter the dog then. She also asked that I replace the missing testicles with prosthetics so her husband would never know about the surgical procedure. This, too, was another hard no.

I texted: *I do not perform surgeries in homes. Please find someone else to assist you.*

I thought to myself, *Preferably someone without scruples.* I imagined, a year later, the couple having an argument and the wife blurting out, "Well, I went ahead and had the dog neutered, and you never even knew about it!"

The prosthetics, called Neuticles, were developed by physicians for use in men born without a testicle, or when one or both had been removed due to disease. They were intended to "improve appearance and to calm psychological fears," but definitely not to bamboozle husbands. While some veterinarians have used them for dogs, I was not one of them. Obviously, in those cases, it was the clients and not the dogs who were concerned with appearances.

Regrettably, all this fun left me no time that day to get back to my book at the salon, but I did return home minus my gray roots, and happy.

As I headed out to walk my dog, I received yet another call from a friend/client, the one I mentioned in Chapter 5, whose dog Sebastian, with the dangling leg, stole my heart. Sebastian had been vomiting and having bloody diarrhea for six hours. I decided it shouldn't wait until the next day and planned to see him to determine if he needed to be admitted to the ER. I treated Sebastian, decided he was stable, and went home approximately two hours later, too exhausted to do anything but watch Netflix.

On Thursday, we had a busy morning of appointments, starting at 7:00 a.m. We saw a limping retriever named Harold who needed X-rays, followed by Forrest, a pointer who had eaten the head off a baby bunny that morning. Next came a nervous cat named Polo who emptied his bladder on Natalie. Luckily, not only had we come prepared with a change of scrubs in the car, but we were running ahead of schedule.

At our fourth visit we were greeted by the client, who sat back in an Adirondack chair on his fenced-in, partially shaded front lawn. Heinrich, a herding breed mix, had always been difficult to catch while in the home. This day there was no garage, and I had brought my leash. I calf-roped him, rodeo style, and guided him to the scale as the client watched from his lawn chair. It took another full five minutes of wrestling to get the dog's weight. The client, a sweet elderly widower who was oblivious to our struggle, did not offer assistance. I made a mental note to bring a bowl of popcorn and Milk Duds to the next visit so he could more fully enjoy the show. He mentioned he didn't need to wear a mask because he had been told by people "what to do" during our pandemic visit. I could only presume he interpreted their comments to mean he should socially isolate himself and resist helping the vet and her assistant as they chased his dog around the front lawn.

Typically, I asked clients to be in a separate area and hand me the pets on a double leash, to avoid social interaction with anyone but the pets at our visits. But this day, I would have welcomed a little help had it been offered.

We traveled to the next appointment, again ahead of schedule. We had received several text messages from a client who had four cats and just adopted their *first dog ever*.

They not only had never had a dog but also didn't seem to know the first thing about dogs, as evidenced by their steady stream of clueless questions. We already had a visit scheduled for the following week, but three days into the adoption and thirty-five texts later, I made an executive decision and added him to the schedule to "answer many of your questions in person."

During the pandemic, people adopted puppies and kittens in droves and fostered or adopted adult pets from rescues. This was a good thing, with more people at home and better able to train the pets properly, etc. Most rescue groups sent families home with a list of veterinarians who offered discounted spays and neuters. They gave training instructions and "what to expect" FAQ sheets. Often those instructions contained bad advice, which I then debunked. However, it seemed this family adopted from the only rescue group on the planet who gave no instructions. It was quite unusual. They reached out to me. Here are some of the texts I received.

Why won't the dog eat?

Do dogs take a few days to eat after being adopted?

Should he eat dry food, wet food, or both? If so, how much of each?

Is it okay if I give him cold water? It's so hot outside.

Why does the puppy sleep during the day? How many hours a day should he sleep? Should we get him a bed to sleep in?

Should we take him out in the yard?

When do dogs go to the bathroom? How many times a day does he need to go to the bathroom?

How many times a day does he need to . . .

I envisioned a long weekend of texts ahead of me. I came close to suggesting, "Just google it until I see you," but I didn't. We met them in their screened-in porch, facing the full eighty-nine-degree sun. I talked so much, my spittle and sweat soaked through my mask. The puppy fell asleep at the visit. I knew exactly how he felt.

Just as I wrapped up my new puppy spiel with the wife, the husband walked in and expected me to start from the beginning. I thought I might cry. I referred him to detailed notes I had written down and said his wife would fully debrief him. We would be in touch with the parasite test results the following day, when I could answer more questions if needed (from the comfort of my air-conditioned home office). I was getting punchy. It was 1:30 p.m. We had been at it since 7:00 a.m. I needed to hydrate and cool off, as it was ninety-three degrees and the tarmac was starting to melt.

I had a final double-dog appointment left. Gadget and Lukey were two large Chihuahua mixes. Lukey was always muzzled for in-home visits but was quiet and cooperative when raised up on a table for exams. If and when the client removed the muzzle, Lukey invariably bit at our heels.

We joked, "Wear thick socks today, we're seeing Lukey." I was relieved to see the client had at last purchased his own muzzle and placed it on Lukey properly. We met on the back deck, devoid of any furniture or elevated surface upon which to work, other than the comfy chair occupied by the client. We were forced to crouch on the deck, examine both dogs, and answer the client's fifty-five questions. Or at least I think that's what I did. I may have drifted in and out of consciousness a few times during the interminable visit.

After both dogs were examined and we were about to leave, Lukey, whose muzzle was still on, lunged at me and dove at my hand, attempting to bite with unprecedented ferociousness. The muzzle worked, and I only received a scratch from an errant protruding snaggletooth. My submissive position on the ground, at his level, was obviously not one in which I had the upper hand.

Note to self: If I was to ever return, I would need a table. Had I not been dehydrated and exhausted, I would have requested one sooner. We departed, uncomfortable in the ninety-four-degree heat but relieved to have all fingers intact.

My workday ended several hours later when all my clients were notified of tests results, prescriptions were filled, and more appointments were scheduled for the following week. Wine o'clock had arrived.

It had been a long week in a very long year. COVID-19 tested every bit of my knowledge, patience, and ingenuity, making me completely rethink how I could efficiently and safely treat my patients without risking the health of myself, my family, and my employees. Everything became more complicated, but somehow, we got through it. I will forever be grateful to the clients who thought to place a heater or a fan in their garage, or put out a table with a towel, to spare us from bending over or sitting on a concrete garage floor. And I know they were relieved to be seen in their homes, rather than having to drop off their pet in a parking lot and await a call from the vet in the hospital with an update or diagnosis, far removed from their pet and any chance of comforting them during a crisis.

Toward the end of COVID, I sold my mobile practice and relocated cross-country. One of the hardest things I ever did was finding other veterinarians to take over the care of my beloved patients. COVID marked the end of the best years of my career, connecting with clients and patients in a way that helped me see that what I did made a difference in the lives of those whose pets I treated. I am forever changed for the better from the experiences I had during all aspects of my career, from full- and part-time in the clinics, to being a relief vet, to a house-call practitioner, and now, again as a relief vet. I'm very fortunate to have the career I did. I met some wonderful clients and pets whose stories have enriched my life, and hopefully yours as well.

REFERENCES

American Pet Products Association. "Latest Pet Ownership and Spending Data from APPA Reveals Continued Strength of National Pet Industry in the Face of Economic Uncertainty." Last modified March 23, 2023. https://www.americanpet products.org/news/press-release/latest-pet-ownership-and -spending-data-from-appa-reveals-continued-strength-of -national-pet-industry-in-the-face-of-economic-uncertainty.

American Veterinary Medical Association. "AVMA 2022 Pet Ownership and Demographics Sourcebook." Schaumburg, IL: American Veterinary Medical Association, 2022.

Bolstad, Courtney J., Ben Porter, Cynthia J. Brown, Richard E. Kennedy, and Michael R. Nadorff. "The Relation Between Pet Ownership, Anxiety, and Depressive Symptoms in Late Life." *Anthrozoos* 34, no. 5 (June 2021): 671–84.

Brooks, Helen Louise, Kelly Rushton, Karina Lovell, Penny Bee, Lauren Walker, Laura Grant, and Anne Rogers. "The Power of Support from Companion Animals for People Living with Mental Health Problems: A Systematic Review and Narrative Synthesis of the Evidence." *BMC Psychiatry* 18, no. 1 (February 2018).

Brscic, Marta, Barbara Contiero, Alessandro Schianchi, and Cristina Marogna. "Challenging Suicide, Burnout, and Depression among Veterinary Practitioners and Students: Text Mining and Topics Modelling Analysis of the Scientific Literature." *BMC Veterinary Research* 17, no. 1 (September 2021).

Burns, Katie. "New Report Takes a Deep Dive into Pet Ownership." American Veterinary Medical Association. Last modified June 20 2022. https://www.avma.org/news/new-report-takes-deep-dive-pet-ownership.

Cherniack, E. Paul, and Ariella R. Cherniack. "The Benefits of Pets and Animal-Assisted Therapy to the Health of Older Individuals." *Current Gerontology and Geriatrics* Research (November 2014), https://doi.org/10.1155/2014/623203.

Grajfoner, Dasha, Guek Nee Ke, and Rachel Mei Ming Wong. "The Effect of Pets on Human Mental Health and Wellbeing during COVID-19 Lockdown in Malaysia." *Animals (Basel)* 11, no. 9 (September 2021).

Insurance Information Institute. "Facts + Statistics: Pet Ownership and Insurance." New York, NY: Insurance Information Institute, 2023. https://www.iii.org/fact-statistic/facts-statistics-pet-ownership-and-insurance.

Jones, Melanie G., Simon M. Rice, and Susan M. Cotton. "Incorporating Animal-Assisted Therapy in Mental Health Treatments for Adolescents: A Systematic Review of Canine Assisted Psychotherapy." *PLoS One* 14, no. 1 (January 2019).

Megna, Michelle. "Pet Ownership Statistics 2024." Last modified January 25, 2024. *Forbes Advisor.* https://www.forbes.com/advisor/pet-insurance/pet-ownership-statistics/.

Opdebeeck, Carol, Michael A. Katsaris, Anthony Martyr, Ruth A. Lamont, James A. Pickett, Isla Rippon, Jeanette M. Thom, Christina Victor, and Linda Clare. "What Are the Benefits of Pet Ownership and Care Among People with Mild-to-Moderate Dementia? Findings from the IDEAL Programme." *Journal of Applied Gerontology* 40, no. 11 (November 2021): 1559–67.

REFERENCES

Teo, Jillian T., Stuart J. Johnstone, Stephanie S. Romer, and Susan J. Thomas. "Psychophysiological Mechanisms Underlying the Potential Health Benefits of Human-Dog Interactions: A Systemic Literature Review." *International Journal of Psychophysiology* 180 (October 2022): 27–48.

Wolynczyk-Gmaj, Dorota, Aleksandra Ziólkowska, Piotr Rogala, David Šcigala, Ludwik Bryla, Bartlomiej Gmaj, and Marcin Wojnar. "Can Dog-Assisted Intervention Decrease Anxiety Level and Autonomic Agitation in Patients with Anxiety Disorders?" *Journal of Clinical Medicine* 10, no. 21 (November 2021): 5171.

ACKNOWLEDGMENTS

I have met so many inspiring people in my career, and I decided that what I have learned and witnessed was worth repeating. I have been blessed with a job that brought me constant variety and opportunities to meet thousands of pets and people, many of whom enriched my life. Yet the book as you know it would not exist without the help and support of several people.

Thank you, Blair, my superb life coach, friend, and cheerleader. You encouraged me to make my dream of writing a book a reality.

To my editors, Michele Orwin and Lorraine Fico White, Bridget Boland, and Sheila Trask—I learned so much from you all, and your collective advice was priceless. This book would have been loaded with clichés, dangling participles, passive sentences, and entirely too many adverbs. I now understand that being an avid reader does not make someone a grammatically correct writer. Thank you!

To Brooke Warner and Shannon Green at She Writes Press, I feel so fortunate and grateful that I went on this journey with you and your industry-changing organization. You are making it possible for stories and voices like mine to be heard. Thanks to Tabitha Lahr for the beautiful cover design. Thanks to Ann Marie Nieves and Lori Edelman for helping pet lovers find me and my book.

I would not have had a business without my house-call veterinary nurses. Most importantly . . . I could not have seen cats without you! Thanks for the heavy lifting and listening to all my stories while "trapped" in my Subaru.

To all my mentees who spent their summers and holiday breaks working with us—your passion, patience, and work ethic inspired me. No one will be more proud and excited than I to call several of you doctor.

Huge thanks to my friends, early readers, and constant support system. Kerry, my "frienditor"/avid reader/sounding board—your encouragement, critiques, and advice was always spot-on and appreciated. Daniele, Karen, Aimee, and Doreen round out the rest of my confidence-boosting team of friends and informal editors who always gave me honest and constructive input. Allowing me to be your vet as well meant the world to me.

I will be forever appreciative of the clients who entrusted me with their pets' well-being. Starting a house-call business like mine relied on word of mouth, and I could not have built a clientele so quickly without it. I loved being your family vet.

To my animal-adoring, eccentric family, beginning with my mom, the GOAT of animal lovers—I would not be here without you. Thanks.

Immeasurable gratitude goes to my children and husband, who endured my long-winded, sometimes graphic stories at the dinner table, and always reminded me to edit as I did so. You were good sports, particularly when living with that gross piece of equipment in our garage (you know what I mean). Dave, Isabella, Gabriella, and Chris—I love you all. And to my four-legged loved ones, Coach, Georgia, and India, thanks for the unconditional love. Ditto.

ABOUT THE AUTHOR

Dr. Dawn Filos is a small-animal veterinarian and owner of Bucks Mercer Mobile Vet, a house-call practice. She enjoys writing about and teaching animal lovers what she has learned and observed over the last three decades. You can read more on her blog at www.drdawnthepetvet.com, and follow her on social media on Facebook (Dr. Dawn the Pet Vet) and Instagram (@dr.dawn_petvet). Dr. Filos is available for speaking engagments. She lives in Arizona, Pennsylvania, and New York with her family and her dog India.

Looking for your next great read?

We can help!

Visit www.shewritespress.com/next-read
or scan the QR code below for a list
of our recommended titles.

She Writes Press is an award-winning
independent publishing company founded to
serve women writers everywhere.